Financing
Transitions

A FAMILY————
BUSINESS
————PUBLICATION

Family Business Publications are the combined efforts of the Family Business Consulting Group and Palgrave Macmillan. These books provide useful information on a broad range of topics that concern the family business enterprise, including succession planning, communication, strategy and growth, family leadership, and more. The books are written by experts with combined experiences of over a century in the field of family enterprise and who have consulted with thousands of enterprising families the world over, giving the reader practical, effective, and time-tested insights to everyone involved in a family business.

FBCG, founded in 1994, is the leading business consultancy exclusively devoted to helping family enterprises prosper across generations.

FAMILY BUSINESS LEADERSHIP SERIES

This series of books comprises concise guides and thoughtful compendiums to the most pressing issues that anyone involved in a family firm may face. Each volume covers a different topic area and provides the answers to some of the most common and challenging questions.

Titles include:

All of the books were written by members of the Family Business Consulting Group and are based on both our experiences with thousands of client families as well as our empirical research at leading research universities the world over.

Financing Transitions

Managing Capital and Liquidity in the Family Business

François M. de Visscher,
Craig E. Aronoff,
and John L. Ward

palgrave
macmillan

FINANCING TRANSITIONS

First published by the Family Business Consulting Group Publications, 1995.

This edition first published in 2011 by
PALGRAVE MACMILLAN®
in the United States—a division of St. Martin's Press LLC,
175 Fifth Avenue, New York, NY 10010.

Where this book is distributed in the UK, Europe and the rest of the world, this is by Palgrave Macmillan, a division of Macmillan Publishers Limited, registered in England, company number 785998, of Houndmills, Basingstoke, Hampshire RG21 6XS.

Palgrave Macmillan is the global academic imprint of the above companies and has companies and representatives throughout the world.

Palgrave® and Macmillan® are registered trademarks in the United States, the United Kingdom, Europe and other countries.

ISBN: 978–0–230–11105–9

Library of Congress Cataloging-in-Publication Data

De Visscher, François M.
    Financing transitions : managing capital and liquidity in the family business / Francois M. de Visscher, Craig E. Aronoff, and John L. Ward.
        p. cm.—(Family business leadership series)
    Marietta, GA : Family Business Consulting Group Pub., c2008
    Includes index.
    ISBN 978–0–230–11105–9
    1. Family-owned business enterprises—Management.
    2. Family-owned business enterprises—Succession. I. Aronoff, Craig E. II. Ward, John L., 1945– III. Title.

HD62.25.D4 2011
658.15'2—dc22   2010035422

A catalogue record of the book is available from the British Library.

Design by Newgen Imaging Systems (P) Ltd., Chennai, India.

First Palgrave Macmillan edition: January 2011

10 9 8 7 6 5 4 3 2 1

Printed in the United States of America.

Contents

Tables and Exhibits

Chapter 1

Balancing Liquidity, Growth, and Control

Throughout the world and across the centuries, family businesses share a common set of challenges: liquidity for shareholders, capital for business growth, and responsiveness to shareholders' control objectives. Let's consider the case of Carwood, a U.S. family business:

Judging from their beautiful new headquarters on the outskirts of Cleveland, the future seems secure for Carwood, a third-generation automotive parts company. Founded in the 19th century, the company has sales of $250 million. Reflecting its strong cash flows, the company has historically paid generous dividends to shareholders.

Behind this healthy image lies a company very much at risk. During the last five years, sales have begun to stagnate, mostly due to lack of industry growth and stronger competition from large and well-capitalized global companies. To keep its competitive position, Carwood has continued to invest in new equipment and production facilities, which will keep Carwood competitive in cost and productivity, but only if and when the industry begins to grow again.

Three family branches own Carwood. At the last board meeting, one of the branches expressed their desire to sell their shares in the company—even if it meant selling the whole business to raise the cash. Members of that family branch feel detached from the business and the rest of the family. They live far from Cleveland and seldom show up for annual meetings, even though they hold seats on the board of directors. Global competition, they argued, requires continuous and massive investment, which eventually would reduce the company's ability to pay dividends and could even hurt future shareholder value.

Said one member of this group, "Let's sell before it's too late."

Another group, in which the chairman is one of 12 shareholders, has no interest in selling its shares, let alone the business. The third and most populous branch with more than 20 shareholders in four families is split over the issue—some are interested in selling, some are not, others waffle back and forth.

Two family members from each shareholder group serve on the board, along with two outside directors who are unwilling to take sides. The board's lack of cohesiveness results in unsatisfactory board meetings and prevents it from making strategic decisions.

Because none of the three family factions has enough votes to prevail, the board and management are at an impasse. They called in an investment banker to evaluate their options:

- *Sell, which may leave significant value on the table;*
- *Stay as is, which may be competitively risky;*
- *Find a partner to buy some shares, which may sacrifice significant control; or*
- *Recapitalize, which may require excessive debt to secure growth.*

In what we like to call "the cousin collaboration," none of the shareholders—multiple descendants of the founder—owns sufficient shares to control the company and its strategic decisions. While all shareholders have equal rights, they have very different needs. Balancing the financial needs of a growing business with the divergent liquidity needs of a growing family is one of the most critical issues Carwood shareholders—and other multigenerational companies—will face.

Family shareholders' expectations of the business evolve from generation to generation. Sometimes the evolution is peaceful and smooth, but it is not unusual for gradual shifts in the family and the business eventually to erupt into a liquidity crisis, threatening to destroy the business. Avoiding such crises requires that family shareholders understand and address the financial forces at work.

Depending on the attitude of the shareholders vis-à-vis control and the timing of its liquidity needs, Carwood may yet be able to cobble together a combination of solutions.

THE FAMILY BUSINESS TRIANGLE

Successfully balancing the evolving liquidity needs of a family with the growing capital needs of the business and the implication both those issues have for control of the company influence the long-term survival of the family business across generations.

The triangle portrays the tension intrinsic to the financial life of a family business as it passes from generation to generation. If family control is to be sustained at the top of the triangle, equilibrium between shareholder liquidity and the capital needs of the business must be achieved at its base.

When liquidity and capital needs drift apart for any reason, equilibrium dissipates. Any tendency of family business

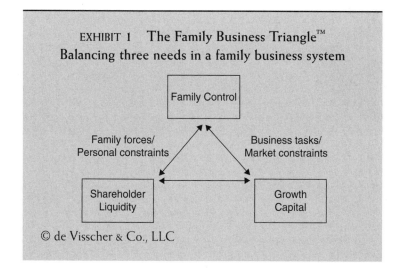

EXHIBIT 1   The Family Business Triangle™
Balancing three needs in a family business system

Family Control

Family forces/
Personal constraints

Business tasks/
Market constraints

Shareholder
Liquidity

Growth
Capital

© de Visscher & Co., LLC

shareholders to expand their "harvest" of the business's assets can pull the left base of the triangle out of position and undermine family control. In countless failed family businesses, the same pattern prevails: Dividends go up and capital investments in the business go down. Diverging liquidity and capital needs pull the triangle apart and family control collapses. (Please see Exhibit 2.)

This delicate balance is in many ways unique to the family business. In a publicly traded company, a shareholder's decision to buy or sell stock has no bearing on either capital available to the business or control of the business. Outside markets mediate both functions. But in a family business, cash flow has to meet both the liquidity needs of the shareholders and the growth capital requirements of the business. A shareholder who wants to sell stock potentially affects the business's ability to fund growth. Conflicts over liquidity or the introduction of outside capital can impact the family's ability to control the business. Channeling family business cash into operations or acquisitions, for example,

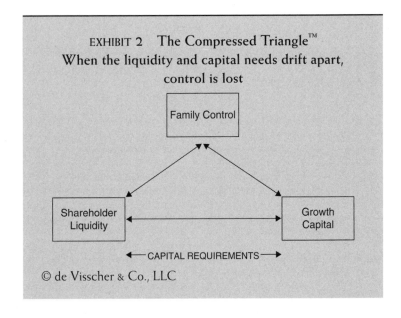

EXHIBIT 2   The Compressed Triangle™
When the liquidity and capital needs drift apart, control is lost

Family Control

Shareholder Liquidity

Growth Capital

◄— CAPITAL REQUIREMENTS —►

© de Visscher & Co., LLC

can easily affect both family control and shareholder liquidity. Change in any of these three dimensions will alter the financial equilibrium of the entire system.

Capital needs of the family business are multifaceted and evolve over time. As in any business, a family business needs *working capital* to fund ongoing business activity, as well as *growth capital* to finance future growth, internally or by acquisitions. Entrepreneurial businesses tend to fund working capital needs with internal cash flow or short-term debt to match the cycle of the short-term or current assets. As a business becomes more established, and its balance sheet more solid, the business may avail itself of longer-term debt. More mature businesses may resort to the private or public equity market to fund more ambitious growth plans.

The business's need for and access to sources of growth capital are likely to increase as the forces of competition, globalization, and innovation challenge the company. Global competition, as in the case of Carwood, requires businesses to make increasingly large capital investments, further straining the business's ability to address shareholder liquidity needs.

Shareholder liquidity needs set family businesses apart from other forms of business. The family business cannot ignore the liquidity needs of its shareholders as could a public company. Addressing these needs, however, will significantly impact the capital resources available for growth.

Shareholders in a family company will exhibit three types of liquidity needs: *immediate, current,* and *ongoing. Immediate* liquidity needs may be caused by estate liabilities associated with the death of a shareholder. Family disputes, which cause one or more shareholders to sell all or most of their shares in the company, can also create immediate liquidity needs. *Current* liquidity needs often stem from the long-term family shareholders' desires for adequate current income on their capital, usually in the form of dividends to cover basic living expenses, children's education, or other needs. *Ongoing* liquidity needs may cause shareholders to press for access to the value of their capital, just as if they were invested in a publicly traded, liquid security. Without that flexibility, shareholders have a difficult time focusing on enhancing the value of the company because the value of their shares may never be realized. If they feel trapped in their inherited family business stock, they may focus on increasing the current income or immediate liquidity.

Family control needs. There are two types of control in a family company: management control and ownership control.

In the early stages of a family business, management and ownership tend to be concentrated in the same individuals. As the business grows, non-family non-owners are recruited into key management positions, and even larger numbers of shareholders won't work in the business. In general, the control objective of shareholders changes as the business transitions from one generation to another, and hence the impact that control has on shareholder liquidity and growth capital also evolves. The more control the family desires, the less liquidity will be available to shareholders and the less capital will be available to expand the business.

> Shareholders must be cohesive, motivated, and committed enough to take risks and build the business for the future—a kind of unity we call the "Family Effect."

With conflicting demands of expanding families and a need for global business growth, family businesses of the 21st century find they are challenged to balance liquidity, growth capital, and control. Three concurrent transitions in today's family businesses—strategic transitions, generational transitions, and ownership transitions—make maintaining financial equilibrium particularly difficult.

◆ **Strategic Transitions.** Continually reinvesting in the business becomes a necessity in order to maintain competitiveness and build shareholder value. Today's family business may need to marshal the necessary capital to make well-timed acquisitions, expand into new markets, hire new people, develop new products, buy new equipment, and invest in technology. Its shareholders must be cohesive, motivated, and committed enough to take risks and build the business for the future—a kind of unity we call the "Family Effect" and describe in detail later in this book.

Without this kind of shareholder commitment and flexibility, many business-owning families will fail to revitalize strategy, stalling growth and potentially damaging shareholder value or even family control.

The globalization of today's business environment has further underlined the importance of family businesses growth. Family businesses may have to fend off competition from large, well-capitalized global enterprises, and at the same time they need to seek strategic opportunities to grow and maintain shareholder value. There are four ways family businesses can grow. (Please see Table 1.)

Each new generation must revitalize family business strategy and pursue its own dream. Accelerating business change, intensifying international competition, and shortened product life cycles are forcing successful businesses in many industries into a mode of almost constant strategic renewal. Strategic planning becomes a perpetual discipline. Innovation becomes a continual pattern. Highly professional management becomes the norm.

As the years wear on, personal security in retirement looms larger as a financial concern, intensifying the tendency to ward conservatism.

◆ **Generational Transitions.** Early in his career, the great centerfielder Willie Mays liked to play close to the infield, hoping to nail base runners from the outfield. The result: his most spectacular catches, glove outstretched over his shoulder, came as he

Table 1   Global Opportunities to Grow

	Existing Products	New Products
New Markets	**Product expansion** Focusing on its core competencies and taking existing products into new territories and countries require communication technology, plus strong local distribution and marketing alliances to bridge cultural differences in new regions.	**Company reinvention** Unproven new products and cultural novelty of new markets make this the riskiest strategy. A family business would be well advised to share the risk with joint venture partners.
Existing Markets	**Organic growth** Growth in existing markets with existing products is often referred to as the "defensive growth strategy" against large, often well-capitalized global competitors.	**Product innovation** New products in existing markets require strong R&D efforts and commitment of the family company. Technological leadership is a critical component of global growth.

raced at top speed toward the centerfield wall—a risky approach necessitated by his aggressive fielding. As Mays aged, he played deeper and deeper in the outfield. Asked about his retreat, he explained, "I'm getting too old to outrun my mistakes."

Like Willie Mays, many family business founders or senior-generation family members get more conservative as they grow older. The math is simple: they have fewer years left to correct missteps. They may try even harder to control the course of the business, clamping down on details and avoiding risk. As the years wear on, personal security in retirement looms larger as a financial concern, intensifying the tendency toward conservatism.

This natural evolution in senior family members' goals and attitudes can clash head-on with an opposite tendency: the desire of the successor generation to take risks and bring about change. Younger managers may feel the business isn't changing fast enough to keep up with the world around them. Anxious to pursue their own dreams, successors are often willing to take greater risks to grow the business. They want control of business strategy, often embracing the continuous improvement advocated by business schools, in direct opposition to their elders' plea, "If it ain't broke, don't fix it." Successors may be eager to invest in new strategies or markets, expanding their base of operation to match the energy and sense of promise they feel. They also may be eager to upgrade their living standard from that of the more frugal senior-generation members.

While the dilemma of growth vs. cash conservation is not foreign to most businesses' strategic planning process, it poses a particular difficulty in a family business environment where owners must reconcile conflicting demands for capital. The successor generation wants to risk business capital on grand long-term strategies. The older generation hopes to conserve cash for security and avoid strategies that seem risky. The two sides have difficulty pursuing common goals because their top priorities—growing the business vs. providing financial security—naturally conflict. In more mature multigenerational family businesses, a similar intergenerational conflict may arise between shareholders who seek long-term returns and those who desire current income. The family may need to raise additional capital to reduce the dependence of the younger generation on the older generation by buying out or even providing liquidity opportunities for some shareholders. That's how the transition from one generation of family owners to the next becomes a financing issue. Without additional capital, these normal intergenerational conflicts may become crises that cripple family control over the business.

◆ **Ownership Transitions.** Ownership transitions create the most familiar and most predictable kinds of liquidity crises in family business. Ownership transitions constitute the natural evolution of a family business. The business's founder may own all of the company's stock. In the next generation, the founder's children may develop what we call a "sibling partnership" where

multiple people share control. The sibling partnership generation may introduce a new phenomenon in the family business:
inactive shareholders. Liquidity and control goals are starting to
diverge between those owners in management and those inactive owners who are not. When the sibling partnership generation transitions to the cousin collaborative, the family transitions
from owner-operators to owner-investors.

As Table 2 illustrates, the nature of family ownership and the
expectations family shareholders have of the business change
substantially from generation to generation.

Table 2   Evolution of Family Control Needs

Generation	Owner-Manager Stage I	Sibling Partnership Stage II	Cousin Collaborative Stage III
Ownership Structure	Concentrated ownership among founder or founders	Emergence of inactive shareholders	Advent of minority shareholder class; transition from ownership to family control
Liquidity Sources	Owner's compensation	Dividends and limited internal redemptions	Dividends, internal redemptions, and outside capital
Capital Sources	Primarily business cash flow	Business cash flow and some external debt or equity financing	Capital needs of the business far exceed the means of the family, requiring a search for outside capital
Causes of Financial Conflict	Cash flow allocation between business and personal use	Dividends to all holders vs. salary and benefits to active shareholders	Tension between goals of business growth vs. shareholder desire for current return; differences over adequate return on equity

Let's take a closer look at these generation-by-generation changes:

◆ **Owner-Manager State: Concentrated Ownership.** The founder-generation family business provides a backdrop against which the advantages and disadvantages of later generations of family ownership can be seen. In this entrepreneurial stage, family control is at its firmest, most intense, and most forceful, placing relatively few demands on the business and instead feeding it with entrepreneurial energy and drive. Ownership is typically concentrated in the hands of one or a few shareholders who are committed to agreed-upon goals. Shareholder liquidity needs are met by the owner's salary, benefits, and perks. Tax planning and cash flow allocation drive financial decisions. Business capital needs are met by cash flow that is plowed back into the business. The primary source of conflict by shareholders, if any, is how cash flow from the business will be used. A shareholder might experience an unforeseen need for cash that could raise questions about draining capital from the business. But generally, this stage is one of relative cohesiveness in the face of the challenges of building a business.

◆ **Sibling Partnership Stage: Birth of the Inactive Shareholder.** The goals and expectations of family business shareholders often begin to diverge as early as the second generation, squelching the energizing effect of cohesive family ownership. As stock passes to heirs of the entrepreneur(s), some may not be active in the business, either by choice or not. If inactive shareholders are neglected or uninformed about the business or feel shut out, unappreciated, exploited, or needy, their inactive status creates the potential for two kinds of conflict over capital and liquidity. They may grow resentful of those who are working in the business and receiving salary, perks, recognition, and so on. They easily become suspicious that active shareholders are exploiting the business by draining too much cash for their own compensation or their own pet management projects. Second, if inactive shareholders feel dividends are their only reward for ownership, they may begin focusing on current income at the expense of long-term business growth. A pattern may be set of inactive holders pressing for dividend increases and greater shareholder liquidity, regardless of the impact on the business. This is the seed of a classic conflict that has destroyed many family businesses—a potential family business train wreck waiting to happen.

If inactive shareholders feel dividends are their only reward for ownership, they may begin focusing on current income at the expense of long-term business growth.

◆ **Cousin Collaborative Stage: Resolving Diverse Family Interests.** The conflicts between active and inactive shareholders may take center stage in later generations of family ownership as shareholder factions become more outspoken. Unless steps have been taken to fortify the family's commitment to the business and family ownership, shareholders' financial goals diverge even more at this stage. Shareholder factions are larger and more diverse and may be more conscious of their power. Branches of the family may disagree over an array of issues, not the least of which are how to accumulate cash and how to harness the business's economic power. These conflicts are made even more difficult by the fact that many businesses outgrow the owning family's financial means by this stage. Additional capital must be raised outside the business if it is to grow and thrive.

The family's role in the business often undergoes a significant evolution by this stage. The necessity for professional management may reduce family involvement in day-to-day management. The empowerment of non-family management changes the family's role in the control structure of the business in a way not encountered before. At the same time, the outside investors, who may be needed to fuel growth, will require new approaches to control.

The advent of a new empowered management structure also may heighten conflicts between active and inactive shareholders.

Inactive holders may focus even more intensely on short-term returns, hindering attempts by active holders and management to pursue riskier long-term strategies. All of these factors can lead to focusing more on providing all owners—active family, inactive family, or even outside equity holders—a fair return on capital.

History tells us that family businesses that strike the right balance between shareholder and business needs most successfully reinforce harmony between active and inactive shareholders, which ultimately makes the business and the family thrive.

The seemingly intangible shareholder harmony can lead to a very tangible effect: lower cost of capital.

Business and family transitions make the balancing of control, liquidity, and capital more difficult. However, educating owners and managers on the effect of those transitions can help anticipate conflicts and improve the chances of striking a fair balance.

We will explore in Chapter 2 how seemingly intangible shareholder harmony leads to the notion of patient capital, which has a very tangible effect: lower cost of capital. Yes, family cohesion and commitment are keys to achieving balance between liquidity, capital, and control. That, in turn, allows the family to gain competitive advantage and achieve financial efficiency. In a very real sense, family harmony can result in financial success.

Chapter 2

Managing Patient Capital and Shareholder Liquidity

Family businesses usually start out small. Sufficient funding is typically among the challenges they face. As the business matures, the family looks forward to the business's growth to provide solutions to many of the financial issues it faces—only to find that business success and growth create new and more complicated financial needs: money to finance growth, to meet competitive challenges, to provide personal security, to reward ownership, to provide for the liquidity and control needs of an ever-growing family, and to develop and reward a growing business organization. Small or large, especially when the time comes for transitions between generations, family businesses face daunting financial decisions.

A growing business and a growing family produce family business financial challenges that multiply in number and complexity. On one hand, the competitive forces require a company to increase its financial and human resources. On the other hand, liquidity demands of the growing shareholder base can put undue pressure on the business capital and cash flow. With all those challenges, how do family businesses remain one of the key drivers of wealth generation?

The family businesses that have mastered those challenges and successfully transitioned through generations share two significant attributes. First, on the business side, by continuously refining their core competencies, they improve their competitive position. In doing so, those successful businesses create long-term value for shareholders by delivering sustainable, profitable growth. Second, on the family side, those successful businesses are continuously nurturing the family's patient capital.

Patient capital is one of the key competitive advantages of family businesses. Patient capital is equity provided by family owners who are willing to balance the current return on their business investment with the merits of a well-crafted, long-term strategy and continuation of the family values and heritage.

Definition: patient capital is equity provided by family business owners who are willing to balance the current return on their business investment with the merits of a well-crafted, long-term strategy and continuation of the family tradition and heritage.

In the family business context, patient capital has more than an accounting meaning. It incorporates all the capital that the family owners, generation after generation, have invested in the family business—it is more than the tangible value of the equity. It also includes the heritage, the association to the family business, the human capital, the values, and the attachment to the business on the part of owners, generation after generation. This intangible value of patient capital is exactly what allows family shareholders to make long-term investment decisions, promote sound employee relations, and let go of short-term gains and short-term liquidity for long-term and sustainable rewards.

Such business-owning families assume that attaining solid long-term growth is worth forgoing certain short-term gains. Their attitude gives a business tremendous leverage to build market share and compete effectively at a relatively low cost of capital.

In fact, even in early generations, few companies can match the family business's potential for investor cohesiveness and commitment. A tight-knit, hardworking base of family shareholders is united not only by family ties, but by shared values, common goals, and a willingness to work hard together to achieve them.

Few companies can match the family business's potential for investor cohesiveness and commitment.

Patient capital, therefore, has both a financial dimension, often referred to as shareholders' equity, as well as an intangible dimension, captured by the family heritage, values, and stewardship. In addition to its long-term investment horizon, patient capital provides the family business with a stable capital structure that can weather short-term financial cycles. It rallies all stakeholders around a common set of values, which in turn penetrates the entire organization. However, patient capital also has some significant drawbacks. The long-term investment horizon of patient capital may influence the family to overlook short-term business opportunities that may have a long-term impact on the business. Patient capital should not be passive capital. Because of the common heritage of their patient capital, family business owners often commingle the family business with the business of the family. As we will discuss in Chapter 4, effective family governance is a prerequisite for maintaining patient capital. As the family grows and

Table 3 Attributes of Patient Capital

◆ Stability of capital structure
◆ Long-term investment strategy
◆ Tangible and intangible return on equity
◆ Commitment to all stakeholders
◆ Presence of family values throughout the organization

Table 4   Drawbacks of Patient Capital

◆ Strategic immobility
◆ Commingling of family business and business of the family
◆ Increasing cost of patient capital with every generation

transitions through the generations, maintaining patient capital requires increasing commitment, effort, and cost.

Family businesses that have successfully transitioned patient capital from generation to generation share these attributes:

- They have a performing family business that is *creating value for shareholders.*
- They have effective *liquidity programs for shareholders,* allowing them adequate return, freedom of choice of their investment in the family company, and assessment of value. In other words, patient capital is not trapped capital.
- They invest in *the Family Effect* and in strong family governance to reinforce the values, commitment, and family heritage.

HOW TRANSITIONS CAN WIPE OUT PATIENT CAPITAL

Many family businesses die because capital or liquidity problems erode their patient capital, which prevents them from surviving generational, strategic, or ownership transitions. The business may lack capital to grow and compete or to meet a new generation of shareholders' demands for current income. In early-generation family businesses, a key shareholder's death may give rise to overwhelming estate-tax demands. A shareholder's personal financial problems may create a need to sell a large block of stock. Or the business may need cash for a critical strategic move just as shareholders' demand for current return increases. For later-generation family businesses, the business may not provide the necessary return or inspire the cohesiveness and commitment required to keep shareholders' patient capital intact. These problems do not develop overnight. They often simmer unnoticed for years before flaring into crises that rob controlling owners of constructive alternatives. Patient capital morphs into demanding capital, and the family business is suddenly at risk.

CONTRASTING CASE STUDIES

Let's take a look at how two third-generation family-owned companies managed their patient capital. The two businesses began early in the 20th century with much in common, including a strong first generation of family owners and tremendous growth potential. But the decisions each family made about how to manage liquidity and capital needs led to completely different outcomes. One of the businesses continues to grow and thrive, providing opportunity for a fourth generation of family owners and multiplying wealth for shareholders. The other was unable to meet the strategic demands of its markets or the liquidity demands of its shareholders, leaving the family with no choice but to sell out. The cases are real, but their names have been disguised.

♦ **Case 1: Donovan's Debt Trap.** The founder of an East Coast–based textile machine manufacturer, Donovan Manufacturing, started the business shortly after the turn of the 20th century. His two sons and daughter inherited his stock in equal stakes, though only the sons were active in the business.

Although the founder was a visionary in setting business strategy, he failed to plan for continuing family ownership and planted the seeds of a liquidity crisis that ultimately forced the business's sale. When the daughter, feeling somewhat disenfranchised, needed liquidity and asked to redeem her shares, the sons took on debt to buy her out. Later, one of the sons ran into marital problems and began to drain cash through consulting and employment contracts. Then, the textile industry moved south, forcing the company to redirect itself into different industries amid all the problems with shareholders.

By the time the first son died and estate taxes came due, the founder's descendants had no means to pay. Their only option was to sell.

◆ **Case 2: The Growth of the Eagle Co.** This southwestern food-processing concern was started in 1920 by a founder who had not only strategic vision, but also an understanding of future capital and liquidity issues the business would face.

This founder also had two sons and a daughter. But while he was still active in the business, he arranged shareholder liquidity programs to redeem stock through installment purchases financed by cash flow. This avoided the need to finance lump-sum buyouts with debt. When his daughter later decided to redeem her shares, the program helped keep the company on solid financial footing. The founder also began early to educate shareholders by communicating about dividend policy.

Training of the younger generation and a free flow of information to all family members became a hallmark of the business. In addition to a board of directors composed of family and non-family members, by the third generation, the family had in place a family council composed of the seven members of the successor generation. A "junior" board of directors was also formed to encourage family members to learn about and be involved in the business. In doing so, the family had installed strong family governance distinguished from the corporate governance. Meanwhile, the company grew rapidly, topping $1 billion in annual sales and generating plenty of excess cash. Today, prospects are good for the four members of the third generation who are active in the business and for inactive shareholders as well.

These two family businesses would seem to a casual observer to have much in common. Both:

◆ Were founded about the same time
◆ Have a strong first generation

- Have a weak second generation
- Possess adequate growth potential
- Contend with liquidity demands from shareholders
- Generate internal sufficient cash flow to meet the business's capital needs

But the radical difference in the way the two businesses managed and met liquidity demands from shareholders was enough to set each on a path toward opposite destinies.

- One used cash flow to redeem shares; the other used debt.
- One had a strong family governance structure separate from its corporate governance structure; the other had no family governance and a very weak corporate governance.
- One educated inactive shareholders; the other merely indulged them.
- One kept shareholders informed about the business and the basis for dividend policy; the other did not.
- One smoothed ownership transitions by training members of the younger generation; the other failed to prepare them at all.
- One deliberately maintained a steady flow of information to shareholders; the other did not.
- Most important, the founder of one company had the foresight to plan to manage a variety of issues that would affect the future capital and liquidity, while the other did not.

Few companies incorporate in their planning the need to meet shareholder liquidity demands.

At the root of the transitional crises of the kind that forced the sale of the Donovan family business is a lack of capital and liquidity planning. Availing themselves of modern management techniques, sophisticated family businesses commit to strategic planning to anticipate business capital needs. But few incorporate in their planning the need to meet shareholder liquidity demands.

The Donovan company failed to plan for shareholder liquidity and made crucial mistakes as a result. It took on ill-advised debt to buy out a shareholder, rather than preparing shareholders to accept more gradual, realistic solutions to liquidity problems. It also failed to place reasonable constraints on the liquidity demands of a second shareholder. It failed to plan for adequate capital to meet the changing imperatives of its industry. And it failed to anticipate a liquidity crisis upon the death of the oldest shareholder, when estate-tax demands dealt a final, killing blow to family control of the business.

All of these problems might have been eased or avoided with careful planning. This need for "TLC" (think about liquidity and capital) begins early, typically as early as the transition from first- to second-generation family ownership. The business needs capital to thrive and grow. Shareholders may want or need the same cash to meet their personal goals.

This natural conflict is forced into the open when a cash shortage develops. The necessary tradeoffs often put a spotlight on long-term goals. Discussion of an acquisition plan might raise the issue, "We can't take that risk because we're a family business. Everybody is counting on us for dividends." Or the need to buy out a partner's widow might force the business owner to postpone equipment purchases or diversification plans.

Capital and liquidity are particularly tough issues as the family business matures, because they so often conflict.

The conflict is worsened by the fact that outside equity capital for a family business is typically more costly than for large, publicly traded companies. Some family business owners meet this challenge by pursuing conservative growth plans, which require less outside financing. While this strategy works for some, it may pose long-term risks of weakening the business and reducing its value. Other family businesses hold down capital needs by asking successor generations to make some of the same sacrifices entrepreneurs made in the startup stages of a business, forcing on successors some extremely difficult decisions.

RED FLAGS IN CAPITAL AND LIQUIDITY PLANNING

What are some of the signals that shareholder liquidity needs may conflict with the business capital needs?

As Table 5 outlines, some liquidity needs are immediate—the need to pay estate taxes or to respond to a shareholder's divorce, for instance. Other forces that can compress the family business triangle are evolutionary. Few family businesses anticipate the gradual changes in family members' attitudes, lifestyle expenses, or personal investment goals that can require cash from the business.

A variety of family factors can spark liquidity demands. If family members are close in age to each other, for instance, their cash demands are more likely to converge.

Business capital can be drained when several family members face college costs or other large expenditures. Obviously, shareholders who lack adequate income from other sources, who are unable to save money or who have a relatively large number of children are more likely, other things being equal, to demand cash from the business. And shareholders who lack emotional attachment to the family or whose family relationships are troubled also are more likely to pressure the business for cash.

Shareholders' investment plans and desires also play a role. If shareholders are disappointed in the business's performance or lack access to appreciate in its value, they may press for greater liquidity. A desire among shareholders to diversify their investment or reinvest their wealth elsewhere may also have an influence.

Table 5   Factors that Tend to Increase Family Business Shareholder Demands for Liquidity

Occasional Factors
◆ Death of a shareholder
◆ Divorce of a shareholder
◆ Personal financial bankruptcy
◆ Business ventures
◆ Other personal financial crises
Family Factors
◆ Weakening of family cohesiveness and commitment
◆ Limited recognition of inactive shareholders to business success
◆ Conflicts between active and inactive shareholders
◆ Heavy dependency by shareholders on income from the business
◆ Concentration of shareholders in the same age groups
Financial Factors
◆ Shareholder disappointment in current returns
◆ Lack of shareholder access to appreciation
◆ Lackluster total return on equity (dividends plus appreciation)
◆ Shareholder need to diversify investment
◆ Reinvestment opportunities elsewhere for shareholders to multiply wealth

For instance, as a business passes from the founder to the next generation, the owners' first responsibility is not necessarily to save and build the family business, but to save and build the wealth—by diversifying—so that wealth can perpetuate throughout future generations. In the process, owners could be saving the family business as well.

One of the critical hurdles of diversifying family wealth is the need to pass on a business family heritage, not just a family business. A business family heritage goes beyond the bricks and mortar of the family business. It is the heritage of the wealth built over generations. Even at the founder generation, some visionary patriarchs understood this well and focused on "total family wealth." In his own lifetime, Matthew G. Norton, a founder of Weyerhaeuser Corp., diversified into construction materials, real estate, and financial management through Laird Norton Trust Company.

Shareholders who lack emotional attachment to the family or whose family relationships are troubled also are more likely to pressure the business for cash.

Another hurdle is persuading business owners that not all siblings or family members need to inherit the same assets. The emotional obstacle here is often based on the strong attachment family members may feel to the business. If they no longer own shares of the company, how can they remain connected and identified with that important aspect of the family legacy and identity?

A third hurdle is determining just how much the family business should diversify. That depends on the number of generations and inactive shareholders. There are no exact ideal numbers, but in general a new business usually requires all available capital just to stay afloat. As Exhibit 3 illustrates, by the second generation, when one or more siblings may have inherited shares, the family should consider diversifying as much as 30 percent of the company's value into other assets, which could include real estate, other business ventures, or a family foundation. By the third generation, when multiple cousins may have inherited shares, the family might diversify another 10 percent to 25 percent of the company's value into outside assets.

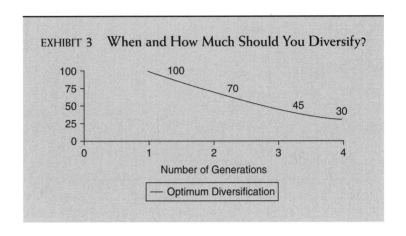

EXHIBIT 3   When and How Much Should You Diversify?

Number of Generations

— Optimum Diversification

THE DOWNWARD LIQUIDITY SPIRAL

The danger factors discussed above can touch off a self-perpetuating "downward liquidity spiral" that will accelerate if left unchecked. (Please see Exhibit 4.) As discussed throughout this book, shareholder liquidity programs, shareholder education, and other measures can prevent shareholder demands from mushrooming out of control. But in the absence of preventive measures, shareholders are likely to demand a higher current return. They discount the capital needs of the business because they see no benefit for themselves. In a family business with limited capital, this can result in a deadly liquidity spiral that drains capital from the business, which in turn causes the business to generate less cash flow and renders shareholder assets even more illiquid. Left unchecked, this downward liquidity spiral will force the family to sell the business.

An illustration of the downward liquidity spiral at its most extreme can be found in the "fire sales" common to family businesses facing huge estate-tax bills. Shareholders' need for liquidity soars and the business is sold at a painfully deep discount, reflecting skyrocketing demands for current returns in an illiquid market.

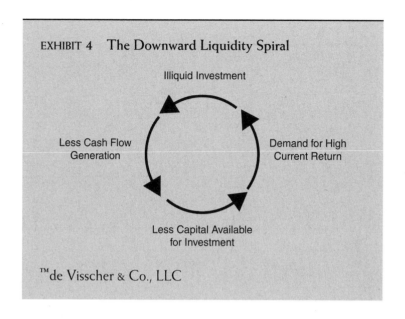

EXHIBIT 4   The Downward Liquidity Spiral

Illiquid Investment

Less Cash Flow
Generation

Demand for High
Current Return

Less Capital Available
for Investment

™de Visscher & Co., LLC

The inverse effect can be seen in shareholders' reaction when programs are put in place to price and redeem stock. "Now that I know I can sell it, I no longer feel the need" is often the response. In other words, liquidity takes the pressure off.

TIPS ON PLANNING FOR LIQUIDITY NEEDS

Some family businesses have successfully used techniques to help them anticipate the liquidity needs of family members. (Please see Table 6.) All aim to keep management informed about shareholders' potential requirements and armed with the information and planning necessary to respond efficiently to liquidity demands.

Table 6   Tips on Planning for Liquidity Needs

1.	Hold regular family meetings.
2.	Hold occasional information meetings to explain significant business events and gauge shareholder response.
3.	Stay informed on family members' personal financial, lifestyle, and health status.
4.	Maintain a family chart or tree to track various shareholders' life stages.
5.	To ease communication in larger families, organize members into intergenerational groups or branches with recognized heads of each.
6.	Keep a comparative history of the business's return on equity.
7.	Have a periodic valuation of the business to stay abreast of potential estate-tax liability.
8.	Incorporate potential liquidity needs into strategic planning for the business.
9.	Maintain a list of advisory contacts and options for responding to unforeseen or emergency liquidity needs.

In the next chapter, we will explore the three main components of managing the cost of patient capital in a family business: shareholder perceptions of risk, the importance of liquidity, and the Family Effect.

Chapter 3

Managing the Cost of Patient Capital

As in any business venture, understanding the cost of capital is critical so that family businesses shareholders can make sound financial decisions. Many family business owners assume that their cost of capital is the rate at which they can borrow money. In the case of patient capital, the cost of capital would be equivalent to the return that family shareholders would expect on their capital. Just like any other investors, family shareholders have many opportunities to invest their capital. Therefore, the return they expect on patient capital should be measured in comparison to other investments. However, as described in the previous chapter, patient capital has some unique attributes in terms of liquidity, or lack thereof, and the Family Effect.

In the following pages, we present a formula for measuring the cost of patient capital. This Family Shareholder Return Formula shows how the three main factors of patient capital (risk perception, liquidity, and the Family Effect) impact the return expectations of family shareholders. The first is the perceived risk of the family business investment. The second is liquidity. The third is the Family Effect, or the degree to which family shareholders perceive the value of family heritage and control.

THE FORMULA'S THREE FUNDAMENTAL CONCEPTS

Before we define and apply each variable of the formula, let us take a closer look at these factors. (Please see Exhibit 5.)

1. From Science to Art: Shareholder Perceptions of Risk. In business, as in life, high risk is expected to yield high rewards. If shareholders feel they are shouldering a lot of risk, they will expect high current returns. In contrast, if the shareholders feel confident in the future prospects of the business, if they understand the strategy and believe that management has a high likelihood of executing it well, they are more likely to be content with lower current returns.

What factors influence shareholders' perceptions of risk? Some external factors can be gauged, such as the company's vulnerability to trends in the economy and the volatility of the company's industry as a whole. But others are much more subjective: How personally confident are holders in the company, its management, and its strategy? Do they believe the company has a high likelihood of executing the strategy? Do they see it as a leader in the marketplace? Do they trust the company to spot new opportunities and capitalize on them? What is their "gut feeling" about the company? Do they feel like riding the waves with it, or deserting the ship? The answers to all these questions can have a major impact on shareholder expectations and in turn on the business's cost of equity capital.

2. The Importance of Liquidity. As with any other business investment, the ability of family business investors to sell their investment and the ease with which they can do so have a major impact on their return expectations. The less liquid the investment, the higher the return the investor will require. For example, owners of a highly liquid publicly traded stock or bond expect a lower return than holders of less liquid investments such as real estate or units in private limited partnerships.

EXHIBIT 5 The Family Shareholder Return Formula
Shareholders' Expected Annual Rate of Return =
$[RF + b(MR - RF)] \times (1 + IP) \times (1 - FE)]$

Definitions

RF = Risk-free rate of return, typically U.S. Treasury securities.

b = Beta. This expresses the volatility of the company's industry relative to the market as a whole and can be found in an investment guide. This number identifies the risk of the investment being priced poorly in relation to the market when the family wishes to sell.

MR = Market return, or the return expected by investors in the stock market as a whole. Historically, this long-term yield has been about 10 to 12 percent.

IP = Illiquidity premium, or the additional return expected by investors in instruments that cannot be readily converted to cash. A highly liquid investment would have an IP of zero, leading to a neutral impact on shareholders' expected rate of return. An illiquid investment would have an IP between 0 and 1.0, increasing shareholders' expected annual rate of return as determined by the formula. Professional financial or valuation advisors can assist in determining the company's IP.

FE = Family Effect, or family members' level of satisfaction and confidence in, and dedication and commitment to the business. A family so satisfied that it expected no short-term returns would have an FE of 1.0, potentially reducing shareholder expectations for current returns to 0. (Obviously, this is an extreme example.) A contentious, restless, or litigious group of holders might have an FE of 0, completely wiping out the family business's core competitive advantage: relatively low cost of capital.

Similarly, privately held stocks in estate valuations are dis-counted for lack of marketability. This highlights once again the importance of planning liquidity programs for shareholders in family businesses.

3. The Importance of the Family Effect. In a family business, the cohesiveness and commitment of shareholders as a group—the Family Effect—is another powerful factor affecting their expec-tations. If shareholders are fighting, they might begin to worry about the future of the business. Dissenters sow seeds of distrust. Even if one shareholder has a controlling interest, minority hold-ers can create enough turmoil to distract management. They might use tactics, either emotional or legal, to "bring down" those in control. If the controlling shareholder runs the business, he or she might be worried about what to do to get minority holders to "buy in" to strategy. Or minority holders might use or threaten litigation to make sure their concerns prevail.

In contrast, if shareholders feel like part of a united, com-mitted team, they are likely to feel less at risk individually. Such factors as family harmony, family trust and caring of one another, family attachment, family pride, family sense of mis-sion, and even family members' enjoyment of one another all can play a role.

If many of these conditions are strongly present, members of the shareholder team can provide support and a sense of secu-rity to one another. They are less likely to demand high current returns. As a group, such a team helps hold capital costs down, and the business's ability to create shareholder value goes up.

The strength and harmony of the commitment of the own-ership team is a critical concept in strategic thinking in the fam-ily business. When compared with the thousands of scattered shareholders who provide the equity base of most public com-panies, the potential business impact of a committed shareholder team of family members with common values and goals is potent indeed. Good family relations in this context are like money in the bank. We call this important phenomenon the Family Effect (Exhibit 6).

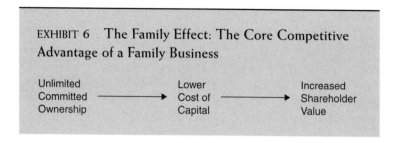

EXHIBIT 6   The Family Effect: The Core Competitive Advantage of a Family Business

Unlimited Committed Ownership	→	Lower Cost of Capital	→	Increased Shareholder Value

THE FAMILY EFFECT IN ACTION

While the Family Effect can be a family business's biggest advantage, a breakdown of the Family Effect can quickly become its biggest disadvantage. Consider these two fictional scenarios from separate family businesses with roughly similar financial performance and strategic outlook:

Company A. Carl, 32, a grandnephew of the founder of Print-It Corp., holds a 5 percent stake in the business, which is in its third generation of family ownership and management. Carl remembers how important the business was to his father, who worked full time as its controller until he retired at age 72. But Carl, a software engineer for a different company, feels little connection to the business, which is now managed by two cousins and a team of non-family managers. He knows few of its employees and nothing of its long-term strategy. The dividends on the stock he inherited at his father's death haven't changed for as long as he can remember. Worse yet, his cousins in the business are squabbling, and family gatherings are increasingly marred by complaints about low dividends. Carl has heard from a friend in town that two family managers are trying to plan a buyout. At Thanksgiving, another cousin quietly began soliciting support from dissident shareholders to replace management. More and more frequently, Carl wishes he could sell his stock, but he knows of no market for it.

Company B. Carol, 41, inherited a stake in Jones, Inc., the family printing business, from her father, who was one of a team of four third-generation managers. In her work as a lawyer, Carol is far removed from the business. But as one of 35 shareholders, she attends quarterly family meetings, where she has learned that the business's long-term strategy is to acquire a leading market share in an increasing number of regional markets, primarily through acquisition. She helped research a family history project on how family values, such as fairness to customers and philanthropic activity in the community, had been transmitted through the generations and manifested in the business. And she made suggestions to a family committee that is drafting a mission statement expressing the family's long-term goals for both themselves and the business. Though an acquisition can sometimes drain capital and is one reason dividends remain low, Carol understands the managers' investment goals and is content, based on results in the company's current markets, that the business stands a good chance of achieving them. And she feels proud when professional contacts ask her if she is associated with the business, which still carries the family name.

Both of the above companies have similar business prospects. But Carl and Carol perceive those prospects completely differently. Carl feels he is on a slippery slope, at risk of losing much or most of his equity investment. Without a ready market for his stock, he is likely to take what he sees as the next best route to keeping himself whole financially: demanding either redemption of his shares or higher dividends, regardless of the impact on the business. The cost to the business of meeting such demands from Carl and others like him seems certain to skyrocket out of control.

Carol, on the other hand, feels confident about the future of the business. She trusts other family members and believes she shares their vision. She also enjoys and takes pride in her association with them. She thinks of the business as a long-term investment and looks forward to participating in its future growth. In both cases, shareholder perceptions are having major impacts on costs of capital. By providing patient capital, Carol embodies a high Family Effect, exponentially increasing the economic power of her family business, and her family, in the process. Carl, on the other hand, reflects a collective shareholder uneasiness and suspicion that seem certain to create a downward liquidity spiral. Left unchecked, this could render the business uncompetitive and destroy family control.

The Family Effect influences the business's cost of capital in other ways as well. One way to lower cost of capital is to raise the proportion of debt used for financing, providing more leverage. But both borrowers and lenders must be willing to do that before it can happen. This is where the Family Effect again comes into play. A lender is more likely to be willing to lend money at relatively low rates to a business with a cohesive, confident, committed base of family shareholders who view the business as a long-term investment. The lower the apparent risk, the more lenders will be willing to lend. Similarly, shareholders who are confident in management and planning on long-term gains are more likely to be willing to take on more debt. Under the right circumstances, this can reduce a business's cost of capital— increasing its ability to compete and to create shareholder value.

Shareholders who are confident in management and planning on long-term gains are more likely to be willing to take on more debt.

BRINGING IT ALL TOGETHER: THE INTERACTION OF RISK, LIQUIDITY, AND THE FAMILY EFFECT

As mentioned earlier, the interaction of shareholders' perceptions of risk, shareholder liquidity, and the Family Effect is illustrated in the Family Shareholder Return Formula. Let's revisit the formula to define its components more specifically and see how it can be applied as a planning and analytical tool. As Exhibit 5 illustrates, the first part of the equation incorporates factors that affect any stock on publicly traded markets. The second part reflects factors specific to family businesses.

Here is how the formula would apply in two contrasting situations:

Case A: A public company in the consumer food business. The rate on ten-year Treasury instruments in mid-2007, for instance, was about 5 percent before taxes. At the same time, the stock market, as measured by the average total return on equity of the Standard & Poor's 500-stock index since 1926, averaged 10.4 percent before taxes. (That includes both dividends and stock-price appreciation.) The beta typically applied to food stocks is 1, because food stocks are as stable as the overall economy. The stock, because it is traded on the New York Stock Exchange and is highly liquid, commands no illiquidity premium. And the Family Effect, of course, is 0 in the case of its thousands of unre-lated, widely dispersed shareholders. Here's how the formula would look:

Case A Shareholder Required Rate of Return =
$$[5\% + 1\,(10.4\% - 5\%)] \times (1 + 0) \times (1 - 0) = 10.4\%]$$

Predictably, the formula shows that shareholders in this com-pany expect current returns to at least match the performance of the stock market as a whole.

Case B: A family business in the same industry. This third-gen-eration enterprise, like most family businesses, has no programs in place to provide liquidity to shareholders, thus establishing an illiquidity premium for purposes of the equation of 0.35. The company also has made no attempt to inform, educate, or unify shareholders. One branch of the family, made up only of inactive shareholders, has begun to pressure managers in the business for a dividend increase and has raised questions among members about whether managers' compensation is unfairly high. While the tensions aren't likely to explode into litigation any time soon, the uneasiness is rising, indicating a Family Effect of 0.10 for the purposes of the equation. Here's how the formula would apply to this company:

Case B Shareholder Required Rate of Return =
$$[5\% + 1(10.4\% - 5\%)] \times (1 + 0.35) \times (1 - 0.10) =$$
$$10.4\% \times 1.35 \times 0.90 = 12.64\%]$$

Shareholders in this business might be expected, then, to demand a return not only equal to but greater than what shareholders in public stock markets might expect. This business's failure to provide for holders' liquidity needs coupled with its shaky family ties and commitment have seriously weakened its core competitive advantage: patient capital. This could cripple the business as it tries to compete against increasingly muscular, well-financed global competitors.

Case C: A different family business in the food industry. Let's take a look at a third company, a family business that has taken steps to provide shareholder liquidity and build strong family relations and commitment. This company provides both an annual opportunity for family members to redeem a limited amount of shares, as discussed later in this book, and a company-guaranteed shareholder loan program, suggesting an illiquidity premium of only about 0.2. It also has managed to build a strong shareholder base like the one described previously in the example of Carol's company, Jones, Inc., suggesting a Family Effect of 0.6. Here is what the formula tells us about this company's required shareholder rate of return:

Case C Shareholder Required Rate of Return =
$$[5\% + 1(10.4\% - 5\%)] \times (1 + 0.2) \times (1 - 0.6) =$$
$$10.4\% \times 1.2 \times 0.4 = 4.99\%]$$

Not only has this company nearly wiped out the illiquidity premium that can increase a family business's capital costs, it has also capitalized on a core advantage of family businesses—the Family Effect—to slash its cost of capital to well below that of its big, publicly held competitors. Again, effective shareholder communication and good family relations are like money in the bank.

THE RELATIONSHIP BETWEEN THE ILLIQUIDITY PREMIUM AND THE FAMILY EFFECT

As suggested earlier, there is a relationship between the illiquidity premium and the Family Effect. To some extent, measures taken to increase liquidity, such as annual redemption programs, loan programs, and other efforts, can increase the Family Effect. In other words, providing liquidity to shareholders can offset a certain degree of family dissatisfaction.

The Family Effect makes a conscious, planned effort as a business passes through successive generations of family ownership absolutely essential.

Conversely, increasing the Family Effect can make up for a degree of shareholder illiquidity. If family members are cohesive, content with their investment, and willing to wait for long-term strategies to yield long-term gains, they are less likely to feel dissatisfied at the illiquidity of their holdings.

MAXIMIZING THE FAMILY EFFECT

Keeping the Family Effect as positive as possible requires conscious, planned effort as a business passes through successive generations of family ownership. Clearly, it is in the best interest of the business and the family to make this effort. Though in-depth treatment of this subject is beyond the scope of this book, it may be helpful to keep four principles in mind: enhance family communication, cultivate a sense of shared interests, educate shareholders, and foster an awareness of shared values. Other volumes in the Family Business Leadership Series (including *Family Meetings: How to Build a Stronger Family and a Stronger Business*, *Family Business Ownership: How to Be an Effective Shareholder*, and *From Siblings to Cousins: Prospering in the Third Generation and Beyond*) address some of these issues. Meanwhile, specific steps that can be used to maximize the Family Effect are shown in Table 7.

Keep four principles in mind: enhance family communication, cultivate a sense of shared interests, educate shareholders, and foster an awareness of shared values.

♦ **Good Family Communication.** Good communication among family members is imperative and can often be fostered by family meetings. Shareholder education at these meetings and at periodic seminars and retreats can help shareholders develop a sense of shared interests. Some business owners review with shareholders such questions as: How do we see the value of our business increasing? What issues do we see on the horizon? What are future risks to the value of our business? What decisions are we going to have to make in the future? How are our industry and the world changing in ways that will affect us?

♦ **Shared Interests and Values.** A sense of shared interests and values also has tremendous potential to increase the Family Effect. Educating shareholders about the business can help them understand that their stake in its long-term performance is held in common. Discussing how the business treats employees, suppliers, customers, and the community at large can encourage family members to think this way. Family pride in the business's

Table 7   Tips on Maximizing the Family Effect

◆ Hold regular family meetings.
◆ Develop shareholder education programs.
◆ Review business results with family members.
◆ Talk with family members about business trends and strategy.
◆ Review trends in shareholder value with the family.
◆ Discuss the responsibility of the business to its constituencies, including shareholders, customers, employees, suppliers, and the community at large.
◆ Prepare a family mission statement.
◆ Set up a family bank (described in Chapter 6).
◆ Hold social gatherings as a family.
◆ Research and write a family history.
◆ Hold family celebrations such as a Founder's Day picnic.
◆ Organize a family foundation or family office.
◆ Develop and honor meaningful family traditions or rituals.
◆ Develop a statement of family values and discuss how to manifest those values in the business.

responsible, steward-like treatment of all constituencies can be a powerful unifying factor.

Mission statements also can build a sense of family purpose that transcends short-term results. For example, some families name in these statements such goals as nurturing entrepreneurship among family members, serving the community through philanthropy, or setting an example of ethical business conduct.

Family gatherings that blend having fun together with learning about the business can nurture all these bonds—communication, education, and a sense of shared interests and values—fortifying the Family Effect across the generations.

Table 8 Four Important Financial Questions Shareholders Should Be Encouraged to Ask

1. What is our total return on investment—the best index of how well we're creating value?
2. How much money is the business spending to create growth and future profits?
3. What percentage of our profit is needed to fund new growth for working capital and for new fixed assets?
4. What percentage of the profit that we keep in the business will Uncle Sam eventually take in estate taxes?

♦ **Shareholder Education.** These sessions also afford an opportunity to help shareholders understand some important principles of running a successful business. Questions that may bring up important discussions include "Where does all the cash go?" and "Why do we always act as if money is tight?" Table 8 contains a framework for shareholder education, in the form of four important financial questions shareholders should be educated on and encouraged to ask.

Chapter 4

The Role of Family Governance in Family Effect

One of the unique features of family companies is the non-financial, intangible return that shareholders receive, what we call the Family Effect. As the previous chapter describes, the Family Effect has a significant impact on the return on shareholders' equity, which constitutes a real competitive advantage for family companies.

Many tools are available to manage and maximize the Family Effect, including:

- A family mission statement
- Shareholder information forums and social gatherings
- Shareholder education programs (such as business education and internships)
- Vehicles for joint family investment
- Family networking opportunities (such as a family website)
- Family philanthropy programs
- Family governance structures (which can include a board of directors, an executive management committee, and a family council or family office)

Effective family governance should address the key roles played by the members of a business-owning family:

- **Family members as shareholders** need to focus on becoming effective stewards of patient capital, determining asset allocation, selecting members of the board of directors, and creating investment guidelines and return expectations to be applied by the board to the evaluation of management.
- **Family members as employees** need to shape and abide by rules of entry and professional development for relatives who have career aspirations in the family business.
- **Family members as relatives** should help preserve the family's and family business's heritage and promote relationships, support, communication, and conflict resolution among the family.

THE GROWING NEED FOR
FAMILY GOVERNANCE

To assume the key roles above, family-run and other privately held companies need more than *corporate* governance policies and structures. They need *family* governance policies and structures to establish clear and formal boundaries between family and business. (For a more complete discussion, see *Family Business Governance: Maximizing Family and Business Potential*.)

Corporate governance organizes how management and the board interact and provide checks and balances for each other's functions. Family governance organizes how the family interacts and works with the business, and it defines the family's multiple roles as shareholders, employees, and family members.

Increasingly, banks, investors, vendors, and customers, who bear some risk in their dealings with private companies, are taking a closer look not only at how the board of directors—especially the audit committee—is organized but also at how shareholders are organized and how they make decisions. Could an irresponsible son or cousin suddenly become chairman? Could family squabbles interfere with company operations? Are there formal liquidity programs to ensure that the business is not exposed to unreasonable or sudden shareholder liquidity demands?

Family governance is increasingly becoming a critical part of due diligence that banks, private equity investors, and other stakeholders study carefully. Customers want to make sure the business of the family is taken care of so that the business can be run without inappropriate interference. Suppliers, banks, and investors want assurances that the company's credit worthiness will not be jeopardized by unrealistic family financial demands.

STEPS FOR ESTABLISHING EFFECTIVE FAMILY GOVERNANCE

Before developing a family governance framework, families would be wise to create a vision and mission statement. While many family businesses have articulated their vision and mission, the business family should develop a vision and mission of its own. The family statement should focus on family values and wealth objectives (building, protecting, and perpetuating the family's tangible and intangible assets). At some point, the family's values could guide the business behavior, decisions, and strategy. As the family develops, there is an increased need to define a credo of common beliefs, goals, and activities.

When multiple family members own shares, they acquire structures to facilitate communication; reinforce cohesiveness; provide for conflict resolution; and articulate and serve common values, visions, and goals. A family organization helps to manage the family's interests and implement the family vision and mission.

The structure of such an organization can be as simple as a process of family meetings at which relatives gather to talk about common interests and issues. A slightly more official structure, for larger families with multiple generations of shareholders, could be in the form of a family council that could determine the structure and composition of the company's board of directors. Wealthier, more complex family business systems might benefit by establishing a family office that operates almost like a small business that actively invests family assets, manages philanthropic activities, and provides professional services and products (lawyers or accountants, or the use of a company plane or the family vacation home).

The family governance structure is a means for creating rules and policies for the family. Many families develop a shareholders' agreement, which is a legal contract that stipulates who can own shares and the circumstances under which those shares can be bought and sold and to whom; how share prices will be set; and how and when family information will be communicated, both among relatives and between the family and the business.

Some families go further, creating a family charter or constitution. This type of document can stipulate how business information is shared; how family members conduct themselves within the family and in public; and policies covering how family members will nominate company board directors, the rules of entry into the company, and many other issues. Additional information can be found in *Developing Family Business Policies: Your Guide to the Future* and *The Family Constitution: Agreements to Secure and Perpetuate Your Family and Your Business.*

In the event that disagreements or conflicts concerning the business cannot be resolved, the family constitution can outline conflict resolution mechanisms, including ownership and liquidity options to buy out disgruntled shareholders.

Families and businesses continually confront unpredictable challenges. Corporate governance goes a long way to help companies—public and private, large and small—operate with greater transparency and responsibility. Family businesses of all sizes and structures that adopt the elements of family governance outlined above will assure greater continuity of the enterprise for future generations of the family.

Table 9   Recipes for Governing Family and the Company

Ingredients	Family Governance	Corporate Governance
Vision and mission	Family values, wealth objectives	Strategic direction, risk level, target markets
Structures	Family assembly, family council, or family office	Board of directors and its audit, nominating, and compensation committees
Policies	Family business ownership, code of conduct, communication, liquidity opportunities, representation to the family business board of directors, employment rules of entry, family perks, conflict resolution	Oversight of financial reporting and auditing, executive sign-off on financial statements, strategic planning, whistleblower protection, executive compensation and perks

THE EXPANDING ROLE OF FAMILY OFFICES

In complex and sophisticated business families, the family office has become a more prevalent vehicle for preserving and enhancing the Family Effect. Those who are considering creating family offices can make better decisions if they can put aside any of several commonly believed myths.

◆ **Myth 1: Only a family who has sold the business needs a family office.** A family office can be useful for large, wealthy, multigenerational business-owning families, especially those with inactive shareholders. Family offices can take many legal forms, such as a family limited partnership.

Especially during times of family and business transition, a family office can help educate relatives about various options, help the family articulate and live by its values, and strengthen patient capital.

A family office can provide significant "glue" to hold together a growing, dispersed family. By providing an organizational structure in addition to the business around which the family can unite, a family office enables the family to see the business and make business and financial decisions in a broader context.

◆ **Myth 2: A family office is solely for managing a family's wealth.** Family offices often provide many services and products beyond investment management. Today's family offices can manage a variety of products for the family, such as insurance, personal lines of credit, business and family travel, and legal services. Family offices can also harness the family's purchasing power, allowing them to negotiate better prices and terms on these products and services than individuals could negotiate on their own. The professional staff at some family offices can review business plans developed by family members attempting to launch new business ventures.

One critical role the family office can play is to sponsor educational programs on topics like the family's business, new developments in the industry, personal finance, technology, or career planning. In addition, the family office can help connect disparate family members and keep them informed about business, family wealth, and other issues.

Some family offices support the family's philanthropic, innovation, and entrepreneurial capabilities. Many families consider transferring the entrepreneurial spirit to be more important than transferring leadership of the family business. This spirit, sadly, often dissipates over time in wealthy families, particularly when the family is no longer involved in management and has the role of responsible family shareholder. After all, entrepreneurs are born out of financial necessity or passion about an idea or innovation. But the very wealth and success some entrepreneurs acquire can cause the next generation to languish.

Effective family governance structures, such as a family office, increasingly focus on infusing a spirit of entrepreneurship, which helps build a bridge between family companies in need of capital for expansion and a growing population of family members in need of wealth diversification and stability.

Unlike great managers or bureaucrats, great entrepreneurs pursue their own ideas, whether within the family business or in some other organization or endeavor, instead of following in someone's footsteps. They generally have three main qualities: creativity and imagination, willingness to take risks, and the ability to follow through and implement new ideas. These qualities can be developed in the next generation through education, family banks, and philanthropy.

Family education focuses on developing in family members the skills, drive, and savvy to assume the responsibilities that come with wealth. Acquiring those skills will also allow them to better understand the need for the family business to take risks. Family business leaders should focus family members' education and training not just on becoming great managers of the family business, but on becoming great owners or entrepreneurs, whether they apply those skills to the family business or not.

The family office can also create a family bank to act as an in-house venture capital fund to support or invest in entrepreneurial endeavors of family members and incubate next-generation entrepreneurs. Such family banks tend to be professionally structured, with outside investment committees and specific investment limits.

Finally, philanthropy is a wonderful way for the business-owning family to "give back" as well as to develop the next generation's management and finance skills. One of the main benefits of philanthropy is that it can instill passion, drive, and ambition in the children, who have less (if any) economic incentive to nurture and apply their talents and passions to any productive endeavor.

♦ **Myth 3: Our business is too small; we can't afford a family office.** The size of the business isn't the most relevant factor;

it's the size of the family and how dispersed the relatives are. For example, take a second-generation business with one parent and three children active in the company, plus two other inactive children. This family may be able to learn and make decisions effectively among themselves. But what will happen in the next generation? That same business family may have expanded from 6 members to 20, with only a handful of shareholders involved in day-to-day management. The rest of the relatives may have spread throughout the country, or even overseas. The company may have grown, stagnated, or even downsized in this time frame.

A family office doesn't have to be a big expense. At first, the office might consist of one administrator to provide the services mentioned above. In the founder generation, the founder's secretary often handles such details. Fourth-generation Freedom Communications, which owns 28 daily newspapers, 37 weeklies, and 8 TV stations, employs one "shareholder relations" person, who actually provides many of the functions of a family office. She attends family business conferences to find new services and ideas for family shareholders, organizes educational seminars, and researches financial and legal resources.

At the next level, a family office can include a staff—a lawyer, an accountant, an insurance specialist, an investment counselor—to provide, or perhaps help outsource, those services. The last stage could be a full-fledged legal structure, a holding company that has some shares of the family business not owned by shareholders. It can also provide asset management, legal services, helicopter services, or time sharing on a private jet. Others manage family real estate, screen domestic employees, provide security, and offer a real variety of services to the owning family.

Another option is to outsource the family office function to a multifamily office (MFO), without having to incur the overhead expense of operating a family office internally. Many families with $5 million or more of investable assets have become clients of MFOs like Bessemer, Glenmede, Pitcairn, and Whittier, primarily farming out their investment management and other family office tasks. Large institutions have also gotten into the business of advising high-net-worth families. The competition among external service providers for family offices has reduced the margins in the business. This has prompted consolidation, producing several large MFOs in the United States. At the same time, services that a single family office can no longer provide competitively to its clients are being outsourced.

By navigating through the various investment products available and outsourcing when appropriate to an MFO or an institution, a family office can offer family shareholder clients the most competitive investment strategy and other services.

In addition to the many positive attributes of family offices, they also present at least two possible negatives that shareholders should try to avoid. First, shareholders might come to depend on the family offices to such an extent that they do not know how to take care of their own basic needs, such as balancing a checkbook or understanding a basic contract. Smart business families make sure that the family office enhances members' abilities with constant education that leaves them empowered to handle life's complexities. The family office merely serves as a convenience and uses the power of numbers to bargain for services and products at a better price than members could negotiate as individuals.

The second potential problem is that, especially in the personal finance realm, when family members depend on the family office to take care of everything, they often fail to oversee the family office staff, resulting in financial harm to the family. A family office should receive careful oversight and be accountable to an active, knowledgeable board of directors. Effective governance is just as important for family offices as it is for other forms of the family business.

By nurturing the next generation's passions, encouraging them to take risks and to follow through with their creative ideas, family business owners enhance the business's and the family's legacies. The younger generation will acquire the "taste" and confidence for risk taking and therefore be more likely to appreciate and support the business's need to grow through sometimes risky investments. Children of wealthy entrepreneurs will also be more likely to realize the incredible opportunity they have to not just invest and grow their wealth, but, more important, pass on the values developed by so many generations before them.

Chapter 5

Keeping, Selling, or Expanding the Family Business

Often, a primary objective for business-owning families is to maintain control over their own destiny. In today's global economy, one question that family business owners face is whether to sell the business, keep it as it is, or expand it internally or externally.

Smart business owners weigh a myriad of factors when considering these three options. From an industry and market standpoint, this might be a good time to sell or to invite an outside partner and raise money for an acquisition or, perhaps, to expand overseas. However, selling the family business involves more than how hot the industry or financial markets are. The family business is part of a complicated fabric of business ambition, family values and relationships, and long-term wealth-building goals. The patient capital that the family has invested over one or more generations goes beyond monetary considerations; it also involves intangible attributes relating to family heritage and stewardship, which many business owners hope to pass on to the next generation. Selling the family business or inviting an outside partner to participate in a large expansion project could jeopardize the ability to maintain the Family Effect in future generations.

Any strategic financial transaction for a family company has to fit into one of four cycles: the *business cycle*, the *liquidity cycle*, the *ownership cycle*, or the *fiduciary cycle*. While these four cycles may not always move in unison, the success of any strategic financial transition for a family business will depend on how accurately the transaction can be timed within them. Let's look at each cycle.

The business cycle weighs the degree to which a company's sector has potential for future growth. To attract outside capital or a merger partner, a company has to demonstrate growth in value and potential business development. Is the business well positioned to take advantage of growth opportunities?

For instance, the natural resources industry currently enjoys global favor because of scarcity and continued demand for energy and resources, while the traditional travel business, with its network of agencies and call centers, has been challenged by electronic and virtual agencies on the Internet.

To determine whether a company may be attractive to an outside investor or partner, the wise owner starts by identifying the macroeconomic trends that affect business growth (such as population growth, rising health-care costs, and scarcity of natural resources), as well as threats to the business (such as manufacturing cycles).

Second, it is necessary to consider the rise of competitors, the development of new markets and customers in the industry, and the speed of innovation. If business survival is in danger, the company should turn to its core competencies, which every business has and which competitors cannot easily replicate; these include certain customer relationships, unique manufacturing processes, and proprietary sources of supplies. These core competencies are marketable to outsiders and can be combined with another business, developed in new markets, or just bought for value. So even if the business is not quite perfectly positioned for growth, future development of its core competencies could be very attractive to an investor or partner.

The **liquidity cycle** gauges the amount of available liquidity and the current appetite of investors to invest in companies, especially those similar in size, line of business, and structure. A successful transition requires a highly liquid market and access to financial resources—either internal cash flow or outside funds from investors or lenders.

Judging solely by the liquidity cycle, the past few years have been an opportune time to sell a business or attract an investor or partner. Liquidity has been abundant. Private equity firms and hedge funds have been flush with investable cash. Banks have been eager to lend and have relaxed their lending standards. Many corporations have accumulated vast amounts of internal cash. All this cash led to many strategic deals between middle-market family firms and larger companies looking to put their capital to productive use.

By late 2007 and into early 2008, liquidity tightened. While money remains available to buy businesses, when liquidity tightens, as it did during the early 1990s, corporate development activity tends to focus on mergers and business combinations as opposed to cash buyouts and investments. The timing of the liquidity cycle will dictate the type of deal that would have the greatest chance of success.

The **ownership cycle** considers whether or not this is the right time for the family to sell or to grow with a partner, in terms of what impact the potential transaction would have on the family. Even if the market and industry cycles are well positioned, the family itself may not be ready. Is the family approaching or has it just completed an ownership or management succession? What is the status of family ownership and family management? How spread out is ownership? Has the family already made the transition between business management and wealth management?

In the *founder generation*, the owner-founder must define the role he or she will play after the transition, which could be as leader of a foundation or other philanthropic initiative to carry on his or her values and legacy. Without preparation by and for the founder, any attempted deal could likely abort.

On the other hand, potential successors might not yet have been identified or prepared. Having outside investors or bankers involved during the potential transition could disrupt the succession process.

In the sibling partnership generation, when control is shared among descendants of the founders, some members may be active in management while others are not. Active and inactive shareholders must share in the decision to sell or to attract outside investors. Their ability to reach consensus often depends on the timing of the succession process. For instance, second-generation members who have recently stepped into management will not have had time to establish their own imprint or develop their own strategy and therefore may not be prepared to deal with assertive outside investors or lenders.

During the cousin collaboration stage (typically in the third generation or beyond), ownership is spread among many cousins/descendants of the founder. The ability to reach consensus on a financial transition without rupturing the family depends on the evolution of the family governance—whether a family council, a family office, or even a family holding company is functioning well. The family governance structure must have the tools to handle decisions about reinvestment or distribution of the proceeds of a financial transaction and the perpetuation of the family values and heritage.

One third-generation family business that had been approached by one of its competitors for a possible merger turned down the suitor. The family correctly realized that the offer indicated the start of a trend in the market for greater consolidation. So instead of selling the business, the family's business council rigorously interviewed shareholders about their liquidity needs, attachment to the business, degree of Family Effect, and desire to pool their assets. The council also formed a liquidity committee and an investment committee to help the family evaluate various financial options for realizing shareholder value. When they saw the right timing in the business cycle a few months later, they were able to handle a strategic transition with serenity and maturity.

No matter the generation, families need a solid governance system to help them make wise decisions.

The fiduciary cycle focuses on the perspective of trustees and owners with fiduciary duties vis-à-vis the ultimate beneficiaries-shareholders of the family company. Those owners-trustees have the duty to maximize the value in a trust—not just the business—and weigh how best to invest capital so as to create long-term value as well as liquidity for the beneficiaries, by evaluating market opportunities for reinvesting the proceeds in order to achieve both high returns and capital preservation within the trust.

The fiduciary introduces wealth management into the equation. Even if a potential acquisition seems attractive with respect to the business cycle, liquidity cycle, and ownership cycle, trustees focus more on the stage of life of the beneficiaries and their short- and long-term needs for cash. The owner-trustee would also focus on finding attractive reinvestment opportunities for the after-tax proceeds of the liquidity created for shareholders. In one recent case, the owners-trustees voted against a transaction approved by all the shareholders because they could not find an attractive enough reinvestment opportunity for the after-tax proceeds that would provide the desired return for the beneficiaries.

Ideally, all four cycles should align when, as a business owner or owner-trustee, one evaluates the potential of a financial transition for the family business. If the business family is not in a good place with any of these cycles, it should consider how to get there.

There is never a perfect time to effectuate a financial transition. However, by knowing where the family and business are in the four cycles and what to do to improve the timing of the cycles, business families can greatly improve their chances of having a successful transition.

SELLING THE FAMILY BUSINESS

After weighing the business, liquidity, ownership, and fiduciary cycles, selling might seem like the right choice. The family might lack capable successors and be unwilling or unable to look for non-family leadership. Sale of the business might promise an irresistibly high price. Selling out and reinvesting the proceeds might offer a better chance to multiply wealth. Or shareholders might decide they want to diversify their assets beyond what ownership of a family business will allow. But there are at least as many logical, although less obvious, reasons not to sell. (Please see Table 10.)

Table 10   Weighing a Sale of the Family Business

Why Some Families Choose to Sell Their Businesses	Why Some Families Choose to Retain Their Businesses
◆ Lack of capable successors	◆ Potential of family business as a wealth-creation vehicle
◆ Lack of capital to grow business	◆ Family pride in ownership
◆ Threat from large, well-financed competitors	◆ Competitive advantage of staying private
◆ Shareholder liquidity demands	◆ Business ownership as a valuable component of family heritage
◆ Estate-tax burden	◆ Desire to pass on opportunities to children
◆ Lure of high prices on private or public markets	◆ Role of business in keeping family together
◆ Promise of greater wealth by reinvesting assets	◆ Fear that passive wealth could harm family values and work ethic
◆ Shareholder desire to diversify investment for higher return	◆ Concern that investing in new areas is more risky than maintaining business

A decision to pursue the opportunity should follow the following principles: know the suitor; control the process; protect confidentiality; and act expeditiously. A disciplined and controlled exchange of information and due diligence will lead to the smoothest negotiations.

Even if the family decides not to go through with a deal, exploring the opportunity will make them more educated about their business, their industry, and the financial options available to them. So they haven't wasted their time—they've become much more informed business owners.

KEEPING THE FAMILY BUSINESS

Family business ownership can be an outstanding opportunity to generate wealth for family members across generations. Keeping a healthy business and reinvesting the earnings over the years can yield sharply higher net proceeds in the future than selling the business would.

Consider the actual case of an electrical-controls manufacturer—let's call it the Voltage Co. This subchapter S corporation is nearly debt-free. But Voltage is not a fast-growing business. Sales, at $50 million annually, are growing at about 3 percent a year in real terms, barely keeping pace with inflation. Annual dividends have totaled about 40 percent of pretax earnings, which were $3 million in the latest year. The business is valued at about $16 million, or five times pretax profit.

Depending on market conditions, the owners of this business might logically consider selling it. The sale of the business would net $9.6 million (after taxes) for the shareholders, and the future value of those after-tax proceeds after 20 years, assuming a reinvestment rate of 7 percent, would be $39 million (please see Table 11).

Why not sell? One reason not to sell is a bare-bones financial projection. Even assuming that the business does no better than its current modest growth rate, as shown in Table 11,

Table 11   The Wealth-Generating Potential of Selling Now versus Retaining the Business Longer: The Voltage Co.[1]

Option 1: Sell Business Now[2]		Option 2: Sell Business in 20 Years[2]	
Net sale proceeds	$9.6 million[3]	Annual sales in 20 years	$90.4 million[4]
Future value of proceeds after 20 years	$37 million	Future annual earnings	$5.4 million[5]
[1]Not its real name		Fair market value	$28.2 million[3]
[2]Assuming 40 percent tax rate and 7 percent net reinvestment rate of return		Net sale proceeds	$17.2 million
[3]Assuming sale price of five times earnings before interest and taxes		Value of 20 years' dividends reinvested	$38.2 million
[4]Assuming continued 3 percent annual sales growth		Total wealth created after 20 years	$55.4 million
[5]Before interest and taxes			

owners could be collectively wealthier by nearly 50 percent if they waited 20 more years to sell the business. In this example, total shareholder wealth generated by a sale of the business 20 years in the future would be $55.4 million, nearly half again as much as the $37 million earned by the earlier sale of the business. And this projection excludes important financial and other rewards of business ownership: many years of salaries and benefits for family members working in the business, an opportunity to pass on family heritage and values to future generations, and the ability to provide significant social identity for the family.

There also are sound management reasons to sustain private ownership. Private status avoids the reporting requirements imposed on public companies. Even outside investors would require some disciplined reporting and could curtail the family's flexibility for employment and community activities.

Business ownership can be a major source of family pride and an important component of a family's sense of heritage.

Family ownership brings intangible advantages too, of course, some of which were discussed in *Family Meetings: How to Build a Stronger Family and a Stronger Business*. Many business owners see major advantages to their families in passing ownership of a business from generation to generation. Business ownership can be a major source of family pride and an important component of a family's sense of heritage. It can afford irreplaceable career and personal growth opportunities to future generations. As a focal point for generating shared goals and interests, the family business can play an important role in keeping the family together, and it can provide a unique vehicle for manifesting family values and goals in the community.

EXPANDING THE FAMILY
BUSINESS

If a family decides to keep the business, members must be determined to compete with other companies at home and abroad. In other words, the business must be prepared to grow or perish. But growth is not enough. Sustainable profitable growth is the goal here.

To be successful over the long term, the business needs to position itself as number one or number two in its market. So the owners must define the market niche they're in and consider how to attain a top position. Where does the firm have a leadership position? Which products or services are difficult for others to duplicate? Perhaps the enterprise has a large distributor presence, a specific technology, or a strong customer base. What makes the business unique and successful?

If the company enjoys a strong and loyal customer base, what other products could it provide those customers? Which companies in those markets could it acquire? If the business owns a proprietary technology, where else could it apply that technology? What are complementary companies?

Each strategy in the grid requires a different type of financing. For instance, product expansion often requires outside capital, which may be amply available because the product has been proven in its existing markets. Financing to build new plants or acquire physical assets in new markets can be obtained most successfully from local sources, such as banks or private investors/ partners. While financing for local distribution or sales organizations is best achieved through internal cash flow, financial entities such as private equity funds, family offices, and private individuals are beginning to finance the expansion of family businesses outside their local markets.

Knowing how much a business is worth and what value could accrue to its shareholders would help business owners to prepare for the integration of an acquisition or to counter strategic approaches by interested buyers.

Instead of weighing whether to keep or sell the business—a question often on the minds of family business owners—it might be time for owners to think of themselves as buyers, or even consolidators.

Family businesses that achieve sustainable profit growth are distinguished by their attention to sound financial strategies and practices. There are seven financial habits in particular that separate the best from the rest:

1. *Establish effective family governance structures that separate family issues from business issues.* As the previous chapter explored, this can be accomplished with a variety of family organizational structures. Where such forums exist, family members know there is a time and a place to discuss family matters related to the business. The board of directors can then focus on strategic issues and the

pursuit of long-term shareholder value. Its time is no longer consumed by family issues (and sometimes quarrels) that should be resolved elsewhere. Likewise, when such structures are in place, outside board members can be more easily selected on the basis of "functional fit"—that is, on experience and vision that complement those of the family board members, rather than on just a friendship or social obligation.

2. *Strive for cash-flow growth, not just business growth.* To Warren Buffett, the single most important criterion in selecting and valuing his investments is cash flow, not sales growth. While sales growth can lead to long-term business appreciation, it is growth in cash that pays off for shareholders. Cash flow allows dividends to be paid and the value of shareholder equity to increase. To measure cash flow, successful family businesses use "free cash flow," which is net cash flow of the business minus investments and dividends. What's left—free cash flow—is the financial bucket from which growth opportunities, diversification, or even stock redemptions can be financed.

3. *Put in place adequately funded liquidity programs for shareholders.* While the value of the stock in a privately held company can significantly increase over time, shareholders usually have no means of realizing this value. The stock is illiquid—they cannot readily find a buyer at close to a price that reflects true value. Hence value appreciation becomes either academic or a source of conflict between shareholders who are active in the business and those who aren't. Without a liquidity program, shareholders feel trapped in their family investment. This will ultimately drive them to demand higher dividends, and higher dividends, in turn, will soak up cash available for growth, thereby reducing the long-term value of the stock.

By having current, ongoing, and immediate liquidity opportunities available, both active and inactive shareholders will focus concurrently on developing long-term financial appreciation and passing on family values. In fact, more often than not, few shareholders want to sell any stock when such programs are in place.

4. *Invest year after year in the Family Effect.* Firms that work hard at maintaining a positive Family Effect face less pressure to provide an ever increasing return for shareholders and higher levels of performance by their business leaders.

The Family Effect is one of the most important "returns" for a family business—perhaps, even, the most satisfying return. There are many ways to develop and strengthen the effect, including regular family information meetings, programs to stimulate next-generation entrepreneurship, and creation of a family-wide philanthropy program. Philanthropy is an excellent way to explore, identify, and rally around the core family values while having a positive impact on the broader community. It can be an ongoing source of family pride as well.

5. *Establish arm's-length compensation policies for active members and communicate them clearly to all shareholders.* The bond between active and inactive shareholder groups depends upon trust. Trust is easily shattered by the mere perception that shareholders active in management are drawing excessive compensation or benefits at the expense of inactive shareholders. The ire of inactive shareholders is aroused when family managers enjoy company automobiles, country club memberships, access to company planes, and low-interest loans, even if these perks may be typical of what comparable non-family firms give their senior managers.

By staying within industry parameters on compensation, family businesses alleviate many of the jealousies of inactive shareholders as well as the concerns of banks, creditors, and employees. Many accounting firms and some compensation specialists will provide data from annual surveys on the executive compensation and benefits of senior executives at various-sized companies in different industries.

6. *Use rigorous accounting standards.* A private firm that decides to go public is often surprised to discover it has to upgrade and make many adjustments in its accounting practices to conform to public company standards. Are there two sets of accounting norms, one for private companies and one for public companies? There shouldn't be.

Table 12   Seven Financial Habits of Highly Effective Family Companies

1. Establish effective financial and governance structures that separate family issues from business issues.
2. Strive for cash flow and value growth, not just business growth.
3. Put in place adequately funded liquidity programs for shareholders.
4. Invest year after year in the Family Effect and family governance.
5. Establish arm's-length compensation policies for active family members and communicate them clearly to all shareholders.
6. Use public company accounting standards.
7. Make good use of global financial resources.

Annual audits and internal accounting controls foster shareholder trust and are useful tools in management decision making. Hire a public accounting firm to prepare an annual audit and make sure it follows Generally Accepted Accounting Principles (GAAP) or international financial reporting standards.

7. *Make good use of global financial resources.* The global economy is more than a cliché; it's a reality. More than ever, family firms need to think globally to succeed. Even if the company isn't yet doing business overseas, its owners and managers need to understand global forces in their strategic planning, because foreign competitors may be targeting the company's once-secure domestic market.

While many of the financial habits above emphasize shareholder value, we all know this is not necessarily the only value for many family firms. Nevertheless, paying attention to shareholder value is the best way to maintain the family's patient capital. Ultimately, that is what all family companies depend on for long-term survival.

In the next chapter, we explore internal financial solutions to family companies' capital and liquidity needs.

Chapter 6

Internal Financial Solutions

Meeting Shareholders' Immediate, Current, and Ongoing Liquidity Needs

We have discussed in previous chapters of this book some important principles of managing liquidity needs and cost of capital. This chapter outlines a variety of financial tools designed to help business families meet liquidity needs in a planned fashion.

The lack of liquidity options is among the most frequently cited sources of unhappiness among passive family shareholders. The demands of these shareholders frequently escalate in later generations at about the time when larger family businesses have opportunities to expand or a need to diversify and require infusions of capital. At precisely the time when third- and fourth-generation shareholders are coalescing as a force to be reckoned with, management resists their demands for liquidity, setting the stage for family conflict.

When considering shareholders' liquidity needs, it's important to understand the emotional as well as the financial issues that often lie beneath the surface. Creating liquidity options for shareholders does not mean there will be a mass exodus of shareholders. In fact, the very presence of a liquidity program could mollify shareholders. Consider these five facts that might be surprising to some family business owners:

1. Not all shareholders in family companies have the same liquidity needs.
2. The more liquidity is offered, the less shareholders want it. Simply offering liquidity flexibility can often serve as a pressure-relieving mechanism. Shareholders may not be so eager to sell once they have the option to sell. In fact, the beauty of setting up a liquidity program is that it helps to unify the shareholder base.
3. When providing liquidity to shareholders, absolute value is less important than the appreciation potential of the value. When a liquidity program has been instituted and a value methodology has been determined, shareholders tend to focus on perceived future appreciation of that value as a factor in deciding whether they will hold on to their stock or sell it.
4. Fairness is a relative notion. Different shareholders may view fairness in value differently.
5. Periodic opportunities for liquidity are more important than a one-time liquidity event. It's more important for shareholders to have liquidity flexibility in the future than to be offered a one-time liquidity event today.

Most shareholders in family companies want a clear idea of what their investment is worth, how it compares with other, alternative investments, and how it can be liquefied if necessary. Successor generations are often increasingly well educated and financially savvy. A family business typically needs a formal mechanism for valuing and liquefying its privately held stock on a continual basis and to intelligently factor in the capital needs of the business so that conflicting claims for finite amounts of cash are minimized. Management can also reap substantial benefits by establishing ongoing liquidity programs for stockholders who want to diversify their investments or get their hands on cash for personal use.

While some liquidity techniques are more useful to larger businesses, many can be applied in various forms to smaller businesses as well. All are designed to help the business owner, in keeping with the vision articulated at the beginning of this book by entrepreneur Sam Johnson, make the most of the financial resources at hand while maximizing the opportunity for future generations to do the same.

PRINCIPLES AT WORK IN PLANNING TRANSITIONS

The business owner should keep five principles in mind when weighing financial solutions:

1. **The best financial solutions are fair to all shareholders, including those who remain in the business.** When a family business plans to buy out several inactive shareholders by borrowing a large amount of money, the company is often left highly leveraged. While the intent might be to provide shareholders participating in the buyout with what is deemed a "fair price," it might be unfair to those who remain in the business and saddle the company with a large amount of debt.

2. **Financial solutions must provide adequate growth capital to sustain a healthy business as well as flexibility for shareholders.** Failure to meet shareholders' liquidity needs in a sustainable, long-term way encourages holders to focus on current returns. This, in turn, leaves less capital available for investment, weakening the business and generating less cash flow for shareholders' future liquidity needs. Sound financial solutions must reverse this downward liquidity spiral.

3. **Financial solutions should anticipate the possibility of a shift from complete family ownership of the business to partial family control of the business.** This step might be necessary to sustain business growth without allowing the family business triangle discussed earlier to collapse.

4. **Financial solutions must be adaptable to the unique needs of each business.**
5. **Successful financial solutions should include information and education programs for shareholders.** This type of communication can do much to enhance the Family Effect, as discussed earlier. An annual stock repurchase program, for instance, can provide an occasion for an annual presentation to the family on the value of the business; its strategy; and its mission in relation to shareholders, employees, and others.

FINANCIAL SOLUTIONS: MEETING LIQUIDITY AND CAPITAL NEEDS

The following section describes 11 techniques for meeting the three types of shareholder liquidity needs (current, ongoing, and immediate). They require no outside capital. Table 13 summarizes them, and a more detailed description in the text follows.

Many family businesses prefer, when possible, to finance shareholder liquidity needs internally. A notable exception: in some situations, a certain amount of borrowing from outside sources, or leverage, is necessary to ensure an adequate return on equity for shareholders. (When the primary capital need is for funding business growth, external financing solutions that require external financing, such as those presented in the next chapter, usually work best.)

In addition to these techniques, many family businesses have satisfied shareholders' requirements with salaries or perks or by tapping the cash surrender value of life insurance. All these techniques can be useful and can be combined with the solutions described in greater detail below.

1. Payment of Dividends

Definition: Periodic distribution of a portion of earnings to shareholders based on such factors as the business's cash flow, shareholders' expectations regarding their rate of current

Table 13 Solutions for Liquidity Needs

Internal Solutions Requiring No Outside Capital	
1. Payment of Dividends	
Definition	*Distribution of a portion of earnings to holders*
Purpose	◆ Helps meet *current* liquidity needs
Advantages	◆ Simple and easy to understand
Disadvantages	◆ Drains business capital
	◆ Does not provide an educational component for shareholders
	◆ Can foster a sense of entitlement
	◆ Requires all shareholders to receive the same payments, whether needed or not
2. Company Clearinghouse	
Definition	*Company acts as an information clearinghouse for holders who want to buy or sell shares—no price setting or guarantees are provided*
Purpose	◆ Helps meet *ongoing* liquidity needs
Advantages	◆ Simple, low-cost method
	◆ Helpful to shareholders who don't know each other
Disadvantages	◆ Offers little advantage to small shareholder groups
	◆ Has no agreed-upon stock pricing formula, so prices set in private transactions may have major estate- and gift-tax ramifications for other holders
	◆ Provides no assurance to sellers that buyer will be found

Continued

Table 13 Continued

3. Company-Sponsored Loan Program	
Definition	*Company arranges for commercial banks to lend shareholders funds using their stock in the business as collateral*
Purpose	◆ Helps meet *ongoing* liquidity needs
Advantages	◆ Enables shareholders to gain liquidity without selling their stock
	◆ Appeals to lenders because loans are guaranteed, either formally or informally, by the company
	◆ Affords younger holders an opportunity to learn financial responsibility
Disadvantages	◆ Reduces capacity of the business to borrow money by obligating it to back loans to shareholders
	◆ Requires company to assume risk that holder may default, forcing it to repay loan to avoid forfeiture of shares to lender
	◆ Risks unequal treatment of shareholders by exposing all to the risk that some may default
4. Annual Shareholder Redemption Plan	
Definition	*A program that enables shareholders to sell stock to other holders or the company within a set time period each year at a price established by formula*
Purpose	◆ Helps meet *ongoing* liquidity needs
Advantages	◆ Establishes a fair and equitable valuation formula for stock
	◆ Through annual approval process, balances liquidity needs of holders with capital needs of business

Table 13 Continued

Disadvantages	♦ Limited by the cash flow set aside in the annual redemption fund
	♦ May have some negative tax implications for non-selling shareholders
5. Installment Repurchases of Stock	
Definition	*Business repurchases shares in installments rather than with a lump-sum payment*
Purpose	♦ Helps meet *immediate* liquidity needs
Advantages	♦ Locks in sale price for stock at beginning of payment period
	♦ Is useful in repurchasing shares in estate settlements and other emergency situations
Disadvantages	♦ It is too complex to manage repurchases by more than one or two shareholders
	♦ IRS rules place limits on installment repurchases, especially when settling an estate
6. Redemption of Stock for Property	
Definition	*Company redeems stock in exchange for a company asset*
Purpose	♦ Helps meet *immediate* liquidity needs
Advantages	♦ Allows redemptions without draining cash from the company
	♦ Allows company to match individual interests of shareholders with property used in redemption
	♦ Allows company to lock in value of appreciating asset
Disadvantages	♦ Has negative tax implications
	♦ Has the potential for disputes if the company still depends upon or uses the assets exchanged

Continued

Table 13 Continued

7. Employee Stock Ownership Plan (ESOP)	
Definition	*Company sets up a trust to buy stock from shareholders for benefit of employees*
Purpose	◆ Helps meet *ongoing* and *immediate* liquidity needs
Advantages	◆ Provides tax advantages to shareholders
	◆ Involves employees as shareholders
Disadvantages	◆ Creates repurchase liability for the company if employees retire or leave the company
	◆ Involves employees as shareholders
	◆ Typically establishes low valuation of stock
8. Split-up of Assets	
Definition	*Division of assets among shareholders, usually through an exchange of shares in sister companies*
Purpose	◆ Helps meet *immediate* liquidity needs
Advantages	◆ Allows company to match cash flow and appreciation of assets with individual preferences and needs of shareholders
	◆ Tax-free
Disadvantages	◆ Difficult to accomplish if business or assets are interdependent
	◆ Has the potential for shareholder conflict over performance of assets
	◆ Requires that comprehensive information be given to shareholders
	◆ May have estate-tax consequences if separation of assets results in higher valuation

Table 13 Continued

9. Recapitaliziation	
Definition	*Tax-advantaged exchange of stock among shareholders to match holder groups' objectives for current income versus future return*
Purpose	◆ Helps meet *current* and *ongoing* liquidity needs
Advantages	◆ Can enable separation of future appreciation in stock value from current income for estate-tax purposes
	◆ Allows separation of voting and non-voting shares between active and inactive holders
	◆ Can serve as incentive for active shareholders by capturing future appreciation of stock in voting shares, while non-voting shares are paid more current income
Disadvantages	◆ Has potentially negative tax implications
	◆ Requires independent valuation of each new class of stock created
	◆ Doesn't provide holders immediate liquidity; merely creates a basis for increased current income in the future

10. S Corporation Distributions	
Definition	*Payment of previously taxed retained earnings in an S corporation to holders*
Purpose	◆ Helps meet *current* liquidity needs
Advantages	◆ Avoids double taxation of profit that applies to C corporations
Disadvantages	◆ Does not allow for unequal distribution to reflect shareholders' differing individual tax liabilities

Continued

Table 13   Continued

11. Family Bank	
Definition	*Setup of a fund to finance entrepreneurial ventures of shareholders*
Purpose	◆ Helps meet *immediate* liquidity needs
Advantages	◆ Diversifies assets of the company
	◆ Offers potential to generate new family capital through entrepreneurial ventures
	◆ Educates family members on creating, executing, and financing entrepreneurial ideas
	◆ Promotes family working together
Disadvantages	◆ Ties up business capital for other uses
	◆ Risks creating shareholder resentment over perceived inequalities of treatment
	◆ Creates potential for conflict over which shareholder proposals are funded
	◆ Creates potential for conflict over repayment terms
	◆ Requires family to share risks of individuals' ventures

return, and the level of current return available on competing investments.

Purpose: To provide shareholders *current* liquidity.

Pros: The most common method used for meeting liquidity needs, it is relatively simple and predictable.

Cons: Drains capital from the business. Provides shareholders no educational benefits or sense of participation in the business. Risks fostering a sense of entitlement among shareholders if dividend increases continue with no shareholder education about the responsibilities conveyed by business ownership. Payment of dividends does not make any distinction among shareholders regarding their different liquidity needs. One shareholder might have larger liquidity needs than another, but they would both receive the same amount of dividends per share. This tends to lead to overpayment of dividends because it meets the highest liquidity needs of shareholders.

2. Company Clearinghouse

Definition: A mechanism whereby the company acts as a stock exchange or clearinghouse for buyers and sellers of stock to meet. No prices are set or guaranteed, and the company assumes no financial risk or obligation.

Purpose: To provide *ongoing* liquidity.

Pros: Simple, low in cost, and does not require any financial commitment by the company. Particularly helpful in linking shareholders who do not know each other.

Cons: Lack of guarantees that buyers will be found or shareholders' liquidity needs will be met. Also, poses potentially negative tax consequences for all shareholders by generating prices on private transactions that could distort the value of stock for gift or estate-tax purposes for other shareholders.

3. Company-Sponsored Loan Program

Definition: An arrangement by the company for a commercial bank or other entity to provide loans to shareholders using their stock in the family business as collateral. The company can formally guarantee the loans, or its involvement can serve as an informal guarantee. If shareholders were to default on their loans, the company would step in to pay them down and redeem the stock provided as collateral.

Purpose: To provide *ongoing* liquidity.

Pros: Available to any family business with borrowing capacity. Enables shareholders to gain liquidity without selling their stock. Can afford shareholders, particularly younger ones, an opportunity to learn responsibility for making regular loan repayments and managing their money.

Cons: Ties up some of the company's credit capacity. Provides no guarantee that the company's credit capacity will be adequate to equitably meet requests from all family members who desire loans. It may not be practical if the company anticipates significant defaults.

4. Annual Shareholder Redemption Plan

Definition: A method that enables shareholders to sell stock to other shareholders or, if no purchasers are available, to the company during a set period each year, at a price set by a formula. A portion of the company's annual cash flow is set aside in an annual redemption fund to finance purchases by the company.

Purpose: To provide *ongoing* liquidity.

Pros: Provides a fair and consistent basis on which shareholders can value their stock. Because annual board approval is required for the redemption fund, it provides a means for balancing the liquidity needs of holders with the capital needs of the business. Assures shareholders of a regular opportunity to raise cash, often eases worries, and potentially reduces shareholder expectations for current return.

Cons: Requires setting aside part of the company's cash to repurchase shares. Requires effort and oversight, including an annual valuation of shares. The formula for valuing each share of stock is based on both the earnings and asset components of the stock's value. For example, a valuation formula might include cash flow, pretax income, book value, or, in the presence of large unrealized gains or losses, after-tax market equity. If not adequately structured, the annual redemption fund could have some very significant negative tax implications for non-selling shareholders who may be deemed to be receiving dividends and would therefore be taxed without receiving any real income.

The formula price is confirmed annually, usually by the board of directors. A non-cumulative redemption fund financed by the company's cash flow is also approved by the board annually.

A limited time period is set during which stock can be redeemed each year, concentrating buying and selling activity

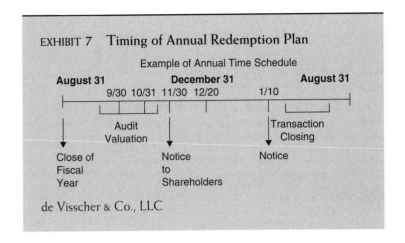

EXHIBIT 7   Timing of Annual Redemption Plan

Example of Annual Time Schedule

de Visscher & Co., LLC

to ensure maximum liquidity. One way to time a redemption program is shown in Exhibit 7. In this example, an annual audit and valuation of the business begins about two weeks after the close of the fiscal year and is completed in a little more than two months. The first notice to shareholders of the opportunity to sell shares and the formula price for the year goes out at the end of the first fiscal quarter. Shareholders have 20 days to respond. A second shareholder notice goes out three weeks later with information about making transactions. Actual redemptions and matching of buyers and sellers take place about six weeks later, during the second fiscal quarter.

5. Installment Repurchases of Stock

Definition: An agreement by the company to repurchase stock under an installment method rather than with a lump sum. Under this method, the company agrees with the selling shareholder or his or her estate to purchase the stock at a fixed price in installments, typically over three to five years. This can be done by using a redemption fund, described earlier, or simply by using the company's cash flow.

Purpose: To meet relatively large demands for *immediate* liquidity in planned stages.

Pros: Provides the company with an opportunity to lock in a price for stock that may be appreciating. Enables the company to buy shares if it doesn't have 100 percent of the purchase price available, easing the financial drain. Can be particularly useful in such cases as the death of a key shareholder whose survivors need cash to pay estate taxes.

Cons: Can be very difficult and complex if several shareholders are involved. Can be affected by IRS rules on installment repurchases, particularly in estate situations.

6. Redemptions of Stock for Property

Definition: This technique enables shareholders to redeem their stock in exchange for an asset of the company instead of cash.

Purpose: To provide *immediate* shareholder liquidity.

Pros: Available to any company with assets that can be separated from the business. Enables the company to lock in the value of an appreciating asset outside the company. Allows use of various kinds of assets, including real estate or even intellectual property such as patents. Avoids draining cash from the company. Allows the company to match the kind of asset with the interests and desires of individual shareholders, providing, for instance, real estate in return for stock owned by a shareholder interested in real estate.

Cons: Can have negative tax implications, with the company and the shareholder each potentially incurring a capital gains tax liability, in addition to a potential sales tax liability for the company. Raises the potential for conflict of interest if the company continues to use the assets exchanged for stock.

7. Employee Stock Ownership Plan (ESOP)

Definition: This technique entails setting up a trust that makes annual stock purchases from shareholders for the benefit of employees, either with internal cash flow or, as discussed later, with borrowed funds.

Purpose: Once an ESOP owns 30 percent or more of the company's stock, shareholders can gain *immediate* and *ongoing* liquidity by selling stock to the ESOP on a tax-deferred basis.

Pros: Can provide tax advantages for shareholders. Involves employees as stockholders of the company (which can be either an advantage or a disadvantage depending on the circumstances).

Cons: Involves employees as stockholders of the company. Not a practical technique for all companies because an ESOP entails considerable expenses, including initial costs for setting it up and ongoing costs for qualification with the IRS, stock appraisals, record keeping, and possible government audits. Typically obligates the company to repurchase shares from employees when they retire or leave the company, assuming their interest in the ESOP is vested, potentially causing a cash drain. Provides relatively low valuations of stock, diminishing some of the benefits for family shareholders.

8. Split-up of Assets

Definition: A division of the business's assets among shareholders, usually by exchanging stock for shares in sister companies or in subsidiaries of a holding company.

Purpose: To meet individual shareholders' *immediate* liquidity needs and investment goals.

Pros: Can be accomplished tax-free. Allows the company to match the cash flow and appreciation potential of various assets with individual shareholders' differing preferences and needs.

Cons: Can be difficult to structure. Can hurt family relations if some shareholders are better informed than others and end up owning the better-performing assets, making essential both careful efforts to inform all shareholders and independent valuations of the assets or businesses involved. Also can result in a higher total valuation of the business, creating a larger estate-tax liability for shareholders.

9. Recapitalization

Definition: A revision of the capital structure of a corporation that enables holders to exchange a new, different class of stock depending on their current liquidity needs and appetite for future value growth. Though curtailed in recent years, one kind of recapitalization, a "preferred freeze," is a tax-advantaged exchange of common shares for two new classes of stock. Higher-dividend preferred shares are distributed to the older generation, "freezing" appreciation of their ownership. The common shares are distributed to younger family members, allowing them full participation in gains from future growth of the business. (The preferred freeze has been subject to extensive IRS scrutiny and has been curbed.) Another kind of recapitalization separates voting from non-voting stock. In this kind of transaction, active shareholders receive voting shares that pay little or no dividends but capture future appreciation in the value of the business. Inactive shareholders receive non-voting stock that pays higher dividends but have less participation in future appreciation.

Purpose: To meeting shareholders' *current* and *ongoing* liquidity needs and investment goals and, in some cases, provide a performance incentive for family managers and aid in estate planning.

Pros: Can meet shareholder liquidity needs and investment goals efficiently by tailoring stock holdings to the circumstances of different classes of shareholders. Can be structured to provide a performance incentive to active family members while meeting the liquidity needs of others. In estate-tax planning situations, has been used by family businesses of all sizes to capture the future appreciation of the company in shares owned by the younger generation; as mentioned, this advantage has been subject to extensive IRS scrutiny and has been curbed.

Cons: Has potentially negative tax implications. Requires an independent evaluation of each new class of stock. Fails to provide shareholders immediate cash for their stock.

10. S Corporation Distributions

Definition: This method involves payment of retained earnings in an S corporation to shareholders.

Purpose: To meet shareholders' *current* liquidity needs.

Pros: Subjects earnings to taxation only once at the individual level, in contrast to C corporation earnings, which are taxed at both the corporate and the individual level.

Cons: Does not allow for unequal distribution to shareholders to reflect their differing tax liabilities, causing potential resentment if, say, one shareholder in the 40 percent tax bracket receives the same amount as one shareholder in the 20 percent tax bracket.

11. Family Bank

Definition: This involves using the cash flow of the company to set up a fund to finance entrepreneurial ventures of shareholders. The "bank" is usually the company's treasury, sometimes supplemented by capital from outside investors. It functions like an internal venture capital fund to invest in enterprises run by family members. Investment guidelines serve as standards for investment proposals. An investment committee of both family members and outsiders reviews all proposals.

Purpose: To provide *immediate* shareholder liquidity and foster entrepreneurship among family members.

Pros: Can regenerate family capital by diversifying assets into other ventures. Provides an opportunity to teach younger shareholders the disciplines of planning, financing, and executing entrepreneurial ventures. Promotes family members working together.

Cons: Ties up business cash. Spreads the risk of family member ventures to other family members who are not participating. Risks causing resentment among family members who may think loans are being passed out unfairly (a major reason for involving outsiders in the investment committee). To avoid misunderstandings and accusations of favoritism, requires well-written, precise investment guidelines as well as clear covenants governing loans, including the terms and timing of repayment.

Chapter 7

External Financial Solutions

Matching the Right Form of Capital to the Right Strategy

At a Family Firm Institute conference in Chicago, Christie Hefner described a phone call she had received from Michael Milken in 1988, shortly after she became president of the then-troubled Playboy Enterprises. At a meeting that he requested, Milken, then the reigning junk-bond king on Wall Street, told her he could easily raise half a billion dollars for Playboy Enterprises. She asked him how she could deploy that kind of capital in ventures that would earn enough return to service such debt. He responded that first you raise the money, then you figure out what to do with it. That didn't sound right to her, so she declined his offer.

Hefner may have been young and inexperienced in those early days of her leadership role, but she made a wise decision. Not only should strategy dictate how much capital is right for a company, but also the type of capital one raises is equally important. Mismatching the amount and type of capital to a particular strategy can doom that strategy. Family businesses would be wise to step back, look at their strategic opportunities and the liquidity needs of shareholders, evaluate all available sources of capital, and then determine the *right* source of capital. The question is not whether capital is available but whether the right type is available.

MATCHING CAPITAL TO
THE COMPANY'S NEEDS

Before searching for outside cash, family businesses should consider the following steps:

- **Draft a strategic plan.** Rather than letting an outsider define their growth strategy, family businesses should develop their own five-year strategic plan by identifying the growth opportunities for the business, the cash requirements to implement those opportunities, and what cash returns they would generate. The strategic plan should drive growth opportunities and the shareholder value that growth creates.
- **Identify liquidity needs of shareholders.** As we've discussed in earlier chapters, family businesses should be well aware of future liquidity needs of shareholders, especially before the entry of an outside source of capital. To the extent that those liquidity needs can be quantified, they should be factored into the strategic plan above.
- **Revise or reinforce family governance.** Before letting an outside source of capital share in the family business's *corporate* governance, it is useful to ensure that the *family* governance system satisfies the family control and information requirements. As the business invites new partners, the family governance should be strong enough to allow a healthy partnership relationship with the outside capital source.

FOUR TYPES OF CAPITAL NEEDS

The strategic and liquidity plans will unveil four types of external capital needs: working capital, bridge capital, transitional capital, and strategic capital. Each type of need fits with a specific source of capital. Mismatching sources and needs will result in cash flow crunches or shortfalls and can strain business relationships.

1. **Working capital** needs emerge from business cash flow cycles. For instance, cash flow needs exist until the company can collect receivables from customers. Typically, working capital needs should be financed by bank lines of a year or less in maturity. The cost of the bank line and the covenants attached to it should match working capital needs.

2. **Bridge capital** can finance either a discrete project or the purchase of long-term assets, such as building a new plant or purchasing a new machine. It is important to match the duration of the financing with the useful life of the asset or project. Bank financing and institutional debt are usually the most appropriate sources for bridge capital. They tend to be fixed-rate term loans, amortized over the life of the project or asset involved. The key drivers should be to match the servicing and repayment of the debt with the cash flow the project or asset generates. Particularly if a project is not projected to produce revenue in the first year or two, debt repayment must be structured to begin only after the project is likely to generate cash.

3. **Transitional capital** needs arise when family businesses face ownership or strategic transitions. Ownership transitions may involve the buyout of some shareholders. A strategic transition would involve taking the business to the next level of growth, such as by developing a new market, a new product, or even a long-term acquisition. As such transitions will result in shareholder value growth, the most appropriate sources of transition capital are private equity funds or subordinated debt lenders. Their investment typically involves some form of equity participation and a relatively short-term exit—typically five years, sometimes more. The key driver to this financing is the ability of the company to generate sufficient value from such transi-

Table 14   Comparing Outside Financing Options

Type of Financing	Need	Sources	Time Horizon	Terms
Working Capital	Cash flow cycles	Bank lines	Less than one year	Floating rates with negative covenants
Bridge Capital	Discrete project or long-term assets	Bank financing or institutional debt	Life of the project, typically less than five years	Fixed-rate term debt or institutional debt placement with covenants regarding cash requirements and asset coverage
Transitional Capital	Ownership transition, strategic ownership, or growth initiatives	Private equity/ mezzanine or subordinated debt lenders	Typically five years, sometimes more	Equity or equity participation, sharing of control, and certain consent rights
Strategic Capital	Long-term value growth	Strategic partners or family business investors	Ten years or more	Full participation in equity, joint control with existing owners

tions, to provide for the exit of those capital sources, and to secure a healthy return to the patient capital of the family.

4. **Strategic capital** fits best with the development of a business over the very long term, such as an expansion into a new geographic area of the world that requires taking on a local partner, or the buyout of a whole branch of a family

that wants to sell. These initiatives can be financed via strategic, joint venture partners with deep experience in the industry, or functions such as international distribution. Family business investors (FBIs) who are willing to partner with the current family might be another source of capital to consider. In all cases, the finding of a partner who can bring strategic or ownership value in addition to the capital should drive the choice of funding.

Before accepting any offers from lenders or investors, owners should define both their own growth opportunities and shareholders' dreams and expectations. Critical analysis and matching of the company's needs with the sources of capital at hand will pave the way toward a healthy relationship with outside capital providers.

FINANCIAL SOLUTIONS: MEETING CAPITAL NEEDS

The following section describes eleven techniques for meeting a company's capital requirements from outside sources. As shown, there is no magic to raising private outside capital. All methods fall into three simple categories: those that involve borrowing money, those that involve selling assets, and those that involve finding an equity partner. (Please see Table 15.)

In recent decades, we have seen a dramatic expansion of new financing sources that are ready, willing, and able to invest in privately held or family controlled companies. One reason is that pension funds, private equity groups, and other financial institutions amassed large pools of capital in recent economic expansions. Many want to diversify their portfolios by investing in stable, well-established businesses. Another reason is that the globalization of capital markets has created opportunities for European and Asian companies and institutions to invest in privately held North American businesses. At the same time, the development of new financial engineering techniques and

Table 15 Financial Solutions for Meeting Capital Needs

A. Debt Solutions	
A1. Bank Loan to Finance Growth	
Definition	*Borrowing money secured by assets or personal guarantee*
Sources	Commercial lender
Purpose	*Working* capital
Advantages	◆ Flexibility to be structured either as a term loan or revolving credit
Disadvantages	◆ Repayment terms must match duration of the business's need for capital
A2. Private Placement of Debt	
Definition	*Privately arranged lending agreements involving senior, subordinated, or term debt, usually for 10- to 15-year maturities*
Sources	Banks, insurance companies, pension funds, or other institutional investors, sometimes identifiable through local economic development authorities
Purpose	*Bridge* or *transitional* capital
Advantages	◆ Flexibility
	◆ Private transactions avoid regulatory requirements for public sale of debt
Disadvantages	◆ Usually includes restrictive covenants
	◆ May not be available for smaller businesses
	◆ May require securitization of assets or personal guarantees
A3. Leveraged ESOP	
Definition	*Same as ESOP described in previous chapter, except the company borrows money to finance purchases of stock from holders*
Sources	Banks or other lenders

Table 15   Continued

Purpose	*Transitional* capital
Advantages	◆ Same as ESOP
Disadvantages	◆ Same as ESOP
	◆ Reduces borrowing capacity of the company

A4. Leveraged Recapitalization

Definition	*Same as recapitalization described in previous chapter, except the company borrows money to finance exchanges of shares*
Sources	Banks, insurance companies, or other institutional investors
Purpose	*Transitional* capital
Advantages	◆ Same as recapitalization
Disadvantages	◆ Same as recapitalization
	◆ Reduces borrowing capacity of the company

B. Strategic Solutions

B1. Sale of Real Estate or Other Assets

Definition	*Self-evident*
Sources	Any qualified buyer
Purpose	*Transitional* or *strategic* capital
Advantages	◆ May trim non-strategic assets or other property not essential to operations
	◆ Raises cash without changing ownership structure or losing family control
	◆ Raises cash without raising debt-to-equity ratio
Disadvantages	◆ Requires new business arrangements with owners of assets still in use by company

Continued

Table 15 Continued

B2. Sale of Subsidiary	
Definition	*Incorporating a division or operation of the company and selling it outright*
Sources	Any qualified buyer
Purpose	*Strategic* capital
Advantages	◆ Raises cash without changing ownership structure or losing family control
	◆ Raises cash without raising debt-to-equity ratio
	◆ Under some conditions, may trim non-strategic assets or other property not essential to operations
Disadvantages	◆ Separating a subsidiary from the holding company may be a complex or difficult process
	◆ May have negative tax consequences
B3. Strategic Alliance or Joint Venture	
Definition	*A cooperative arrangement between two or more companies that pool resources to pursue a common strategy*
Sources	Other family businesses or other companies in North America or overseas; financial groups with compatible assets
Purpose	*Strategic* capital
Advantages	◆ Shared risk with future generations
	◆ Leverages differing resources and capabilities or partners
	◆ Extends partners' geographic reach
	◆ Provides relatively low-cost capital because of mutual advantages to partners
	◆ Can ease access to outside management

Table 15 Continued

Disadvantages	• Requires realistic feasibility study and risk analysis
	• Requires extensive due diligence
	• Requires clear definition of partners' roles
	• Breakdown in trust or communication can jeopardize arrangement
B4. Split-offs and Spin-offs	
Definition	*Using outside capital to split up some of the assets of the company or spin them off to the shareholders*
Sources	Individuals or other outside investors
Purpose	*Transitional* or *strategic* capital
Advantages	• Leverages family business capabilities using outside capital
	• Allows family control
Disadvantages	• May be difficult to attract syndication partners
	• Relationships must be structured carefully with defining roles and shared risks
C. Equity Solutions	
C1. Private Equity Investments	
Definition	*Equity investment by an individual or other entity*
Sources	Acquaintances, relatives, pension funds, insurance companies, equity investment funds, mezzanine funds, banks
Purpose	*Transitional* capital

Continued

Table 15 Continued

Advantages	• Allows family control
	• Flexible in structure
	• Less expensive to structure than IPO
	• Minority partner may provide an ongoing market for family stock
Disadvantages	• Investor may require rights to take control if certain targets are not met
	• Investor may require option to be bought by a certain time
	• Antidilution provisions may restrict issuance of new stock
	• Typically requires higher ongoing rate of total return to investor than the public market

C2. Initial Public Offering of Subsidiary

Definition	*Incorporating a division or operation of the company and offering stock in it to the public*
Sources	Public markets via investment bankers (transitional)
Purpose	*Transitional* capital
Advantages	• Allows company to tap public markets without taking the whole company public
	• Creates a new "acquisition currency" for the family business, which can be used to make acquisitions to buy other assets
Disadvantages	• Separating a subsidiary from the holding company may be a complex or difficult process
	• May have negative tax consequences
	• Available subsidiaries may not be large enough for IPO
	• Regulatory requirements associated with IPO can be costly or burdensome

Table 15   Continued

C3. Joint Venturing of Assets	
Definition	*Equity investment in selected assets of the business by an individual or financial entity*
Sources	Acquaintances, relatives, pension funds, insurance companies, equity investment funds, venture capital funds, banks
Purpose	*Transitional* and *strategic* capital
Advantages	◆ Flexible financing tool
	◆ Partner may provide an ongoing source of liquidity for shareholders
	◆ Allows family control
Disadvantages	◆ May be difficult to attract a joint venture partner
	◆ Investor may require right to take control if targets are not met

a proliferation of sophisticated financial instruments have provided vehicles for this investment trend.

Let's take a more detailed look at the techniques listed in Table 15.

A. DEBT SOLUTIONS

A1. Bank Loan to Finance Growth

Definition: This involves borrowing money from a commercial lender in the form of either a revolving credit or a term loan. The debt is typically secured either by assets or by a personal guarantee.

Purpose: To provide business capital.

Pros: A flexible and accessible financing tool.

Cons: To hold down borrowing costs, requires matching the term of the loan to the nature of the investment being made. (Many family businesses make the mistake of financing long-term investments with short-term credit lines, causing potential cash flow problems when the money must be repaid before the investment begins to show a return.)

A2. Private Placement of Debt

Definition: This typically involves borrowing money privately from financial institutions in the form of senior or subordinated debt or a revolving credit line. Lenders might include banks, insurance companies, pension funds, other institutional investors, or even individuals willing to become involved in this way with smaller businesses. Maturities of term loans usually range from 10 to 15 years, and interest rates typically float in relation to an index such as the prime rate.

Purpose: Capital to be used for a wide range of purposes.

Pros: Offers many options in structuring debt to meet the needs of the business.

Cons: Typically places on the borrower restrictive covenants that can be quite rigid, including terms and repayment schedules. May require securitization of assets or personal guarantees.

A3. Leveraged ESOP

Definition: This method has all the same characteristics as the ESOP described earlier, except that it involves borrowing money from a bank or other lender to finance purchase of stock from shareholders.

A4. Leveraged Recapitalization

Definition: This technique has all the same characteristics as the recapitalization described earlier, except that it entails borrowing money to execute the restructuring.

B. STRATEGIC SOLUTIONS

B1. Sale of Real Estate or Other Assets

Definition: This technique entails divesting assets to raise business capital. Amid signs of a fundamental shift toward flat or falling prices for commercial real state in many regions of North America, many companies are selling real estate in particular.

Pros: Fits well with a strategy of trimming non-strategic assets. Has the advantage of raising cash without changing the business's ownership structure or debt ratios. Can eliminate distractions for management, helping focus attention on core operating businesses.

Cons: Often requires making new leasing or other arrangements with new owners of the assets, potentially raising new hurdles.

B2. Sale of Subsidiary

Definition: This technique involves sale of a business unit.

Purpose: Raising cash for business capital or to meet liquidity needs.

Pros: Permits continuation of family control of the main business.

Cons: May be difficult to separate a division or operation for sale. May create unforeseen tax liabilities or have negative implications for future business relationships.

B3. Strategic Alliance or Joint Venture

Definition: This technique involves attracting outside investors to certain assets of the company, such as a piece of real estate or a marketing organization.

Purpose: To raise capital without diluting family control of the main business.

Pros: A highly flexible financing tool.

Cons: Can pose difficulties in finding an outside partner who sees similar synergies and value in a particular joint venture. As in the case of all ventures that involve outside partners, there is a risk of opening the door to a financially strong entity that might eventually find a way to assume control.

B4. Split-offs and Spin-offs

Definition: This technique involves finding outside partners to provide capital to set up new branches, outlets, or stores that will be operated by the family business.

Purpose: Provides capital for business expansion.

Pros: Leverages the capabilities of the business without assuming all the risk of new operations. Allows family to maintain control of the business.

Cons: May be difficult to find syndication partners with the necessary financial strength, integrity, and commitment. Must be structured carefully, with attention to the same wide range of issues that arise with any outside equity investor.

C. EQUITY SOLUTIONS

C1. Private Equity Investments

Definition: This method involves transferring stock to an individual or other investor, ranging from a relative or friend to another family business, a pension fund, insurance company, venture capital fund, or other financial entity. Private equity agreements typically convey to the investor preferred stock that is convertible to common stock at a one-for-one ratio and provide dividends, representation on the company's board, and rights to financial information, among other things. Private equity can come from various sources depending on the size of the family business. Individual investors or regional venture capitalists may be an appropriate source for smaller firms. On the other hand, larger companies would typically turn to financial institutions such as insurance companies or pension funds.

Purpose: Provides capital for a wide range of business purposes, including shareholder liquidity.

Pros: Allows access to a private equity market that has grown to an estimated $3 billion to $5 billion in North America and overseas. Affords liquidity while sustaining family control. Allows flexibility, providing primary capital for use to create immediate liquidity; or secondary capital to replace capital provided by existing shareholders; or both. Costs less and is less onerous to structure than is a public offering. Engenders a minority partner relationship that may provide a variety of resources, from support for the business's long-term strategy to an ongoing market for family members' stock.

Cons: Subjects the business to expectations among most private investors of higher total returns than earned by either lenders or public stockholders. Poses other potentially restrictive terms: private partners may ask to take control of the business if certain targets are not met; they may require options obligating the company to buy them out by a certain time; and they may require antidilution provisions that restrict issues of new stock. Also, it raises the risk that a financially strong partner may eventually be able to acquire a controlling interest in the company by gradually buying up family members' shares.

C2. Initial Public Offering of Subsidiary

Definition: This technique involves incorporating a division or operation of the company as a separate subsidiary, then selling stock in it to the public.

Purpose: Provides capital for a wide range of uses.

Pros: Allows access to public capital markets without taking the whole company public. Creates a new "acquisition currency" for the family in the form of a public stock that can be used as exchange for other assets or acquisitions.

Cons: May be difficult to separate a division or operation from the parent company. Can have negative tax implications. Requires offering of a unit that is large enough to go public—a threshold that has been rising in recent years. As in any public offering, entails significant fees and registration and disclosure requirements.

C3. Joint Venturing of Assets

Definition: Long popular in Europe and Japan, joint ventures and strategic alliances are growing in North America as well. These agreements allow two or more companies to pool resources to pursue a common strategy for mutual benefit. Prospective partners include any business entity, including other family businesses, with compatible industrial assets and complementary characteristics. Typically, joint ventures involve shared funding of a project, while strategic alliances, a closer kind of linkage, involve shared ownership of equity and resources associated with the project.

Purpose: Enables the company to pursue opportunities that it would be unable to pursue alone.

Pros: Allows the company to build strengths in more business areas than the company is capable of developing alone. Provides access to capital at relatively low cost because both partners see synergies to be gained, including leveraging partners' differing capabilities, market knowledge, management skill, and capital to the benefit of both. Eases access to outside management, assuming that the partners form a holding company that recruits outside managers for the project. If a family business partners with another family business, it can create what might be called an "External Family Effect," with both partners more likely than non-family businesses to share a certain "worldview," including a commitment to long-term strategies, goals, and values. In addition, the "Internal Family Effect" discussed earlier can increase the likelihood that shareholders of both partners will demand lower short-term returns in pursuit of shared long-term goals.

Cons: Requires careful planning, including a realistic feasibility study, analyses of business risk, careful budgeting, due diligence work, and agreements to split rewards fairly based on risk and performance. Poses many potential pitfalls, including a failure to trust or communicate; overpossessiveness by one partner; vague objective and goals; and a failure to attract the best managers.

Chapter 8

Private Equity as a Growing Source of Capital

In the previous chapter, we described 11 ways to raise external capital for growth. Because of the increasing availability of private equity capital for family companies, this chapter will explore the private equity solution in much greater depth.

Until recently, family businesses were of little interest to private equity funds. Most funds did not have the resources to get involved in family squabbles, long histories of low growth, and management challenges. Increasingly, private equity investors are realizing that family firms represent a very lucrative investment for several reasons. First, family businesses represent a solid foundation of operations with a long operating history. They can have a high-quality asset base, established and trusted brand names, and conservative financial structures. Family businesses that have professionalized the business may promise attractive growth opportunities by being poised to capture untapped operating performance potential, broaden their board's strategic vision, and even diversify their financial sourcing opportunities.

The private equity market consists primarily of pools of funds from institutional investors, such as public or corporate pension funds, foundations, bank holding companies, or insurance companies—and recently from wealthy individuals and families.

The new breed of private equity, funded primarily by family offices and wealthy individuals, is more attractive to family businesses than are traditional institutional private equity investors. The advantage of these new private equity investors is that they inherently understand family businesses and the intricacies of expanding a business while adapting to the evolution of a family. Their investment time horizon is longer than those of institutional private equity investors, and in some cases, they may accept a minority role, acting as a true partner to the founding family.

WHEN TO TAP PRIVATE EQUITY

Under what circumstances should family businesses consider tapping private equity? The answer depends on how they plan to spend the proceeds. Are they hoping to provide liquidity to get some chips off the table? Would they like to sell the entire business for succession or strategic reasons? Or do they want to take advantage of an expansion opportunity?

For a family business, private equity can be more attractive than other external sources of capital. Unlike venture or angel capital, which is primarily used for funding growth, private equity also can be used to satisfy the immediate and sometimes ongoing liquidity needs of shareholders. As opposed to bank financing, private equity strengthens the balance sheet of family companies, leaving open the possibility of future borrowing if needed. A private equity partner, particularly a family office, can also offer assistance with strategy, acquisitions, and management recruitment and can even provide further financial resources to the family business. Finally, a private equity partner can become a very useful agent of change. By partnering with the family, this new coinvestor may stimulate improved corporate governance, provide financial discipline to the business, and bring innovation to its management methods.

For the most part, private equity investors are interested in the growth of the company. They are in the business of building a portfolio of investments that must grow to create value for the limited partners and must be realized in a reasonable time frame.

Private equity investors are not likely to invest in family companies solely to provide dividends or buy out existing owners. In those instances, their capital is not used to finance growth. Private equity investors typically expect to exit their investment within three to seven years at a healthy multiple of their original investment. The funding of liquidity programs alone is not likely to generate such returns. However, private equity funds are very well equipped to provide capital to finance a growth plan or to fund an acquisition—even in combination with a liquidity event.

Here are two examples of how private equity helped two companies meet their growth and family goals:

- ◆ **Financing Aggressive Growth.** Five years ago, a landscaping company in the Midwest with annual revenues of $40 million developed an aggressive growth plan to expand its business into several new locations. To finance this expansion, the family shareholders decided to recapitalize the company, including an injection of $12 million in new private equity capital: $10 million to finance the expansion and $2 million to provide some liquidity for the eight family owners. After the recapitalization was completed, the family's stake in the company declined from 100 percent to 40 percent; the private equity partner owned the remaining 60 percent.

  The family members continued to manage the company successfully. After three years, they were able to recapitalize again—this time with debt—to buy out the private equity investors and go back to a control position, while returning about $24 million to the private equity fund. Today, the company has doubled in size. It will use its expanded cash flow to repay the debt.

- ◆ **Buying Out Embattled Shareholders.** In the second example, two branches of a second-generation, Canada-based commercial real estate company had battled for 12 years over the strategy of the business—in particular over opportunities to develop hospitality properties in Florida. A series of animated board discussions between the two family factions resulted in the stalling of other pressing business decisions. The showdown came when the reluctant faction expressed the desire to sell out. With the help of a financial advisor, the progrowth group identified potential private equity partners to provide funding for the buyout while offering their experience and funds to assist in the Florida growth plans.

In the end, the company consummated its transaction with a private equity partner and began developing the properties in Florida. Three years later, the Florida project was so successful that the family was able to buy out the private equity partner with the proceeds of the sale of only one of the hotel properties.

SOME DRAWBACKS

There are some drawbacks to private equity in a family company. First, such investors will not help solve diverging liquidity needs of shareholders and may sometimes limit the timing and opportunity for liquidity by the family. They may also infringe on family business control by their participation in management and their access to information.

In general, because the investment horizon of the family's patient capital will always be longer than the investment horizon of private equity investors, irrespective of their type, family business owners should view private equity as a source of transitional capital rather than permanent capital. Private equity is useful to effectuate a strategic or ownership transition in the business. However, when inviting a private equity partner as an investor in the family business, the family should plan the timing and the method of the partner's exit.

Think of private equity as transitional capital. In most cases, a family's patient capital will outlive the investment period of a private equity partner. Planning for the exit of the private equity investor after the transition is completed is as important as attracting the right partner at the outset.

With the growth and maturity of the private equity market, the alternatives for family businesses are multiplying every day. The question for many family businesses, therefore, is not whether but how to attract the right partner. Here are some guidelines to help determine whether the partner is a good match.

GENERAL DUE DILIGENCE

◆ **Chemistry and trust.** As is true of any partnership, a private equity relationship must be developed on the basis of mutual trust and respect. Conduct extensive research on the managers of the fund—their background, reputation, and integrity.

◆ **Knowledge of the industry.** Capital is not the only benefit private equity partners should offer. They should also help implement the company's growth plans. Therefore, it pays to find a partner who knows the industry and has contacts within it.

◆ **Experience with family businesses and how they operate.** An ideal partner understands and can relate to family business issues: shareholder liquidity and control, family governance, family culture and heritage, attachment to the community. It pays to investigate and evaluate a potential partner's past investments in family companies.

◆ **Track record and general reputation.** The private equity literature—journals, newsletters, and Internet resources—can provide some idea of returns in the industry, which family business owners can compare with a potential partner's track record. It's also important to look behind the numbers by examining the quality of the firm's investments. What is its reputation in the investment world? It's best to work with a fund that is in good standing with institutions and investors. A good partner is one that has been supportive of its investments, even when the financial performance has not been as expected.

STRUCTURE OF THE FUND

◆ **Size.** The size of the fund determines the amount of capital the fund is looking to invest in individual companies to maintain a diversified portfolio. The fund should be small enough that its investment in the family company is important to the investors. For instance, a family business looking for a $10 million investment would not want a $500 million fund, which would consider the amount it's investing in the family company to be so small that it's not worth their attention.

Similarly, the fund should not be too small. If a family business needs more money down the road, the investors should have the capital to provide it. A $20 million private equity fund might make five to seven investments of $3 million to $5 million. A $1 billion fund may make ten investments of $100 million or more. As a general guideline, the fund's investment in the family company should not represent less than 5 percent or more than 25 percent of its portfolio.

◆ **Governance structure.** Most private equity funds consist of several professional investment partners and are managed by a general partner. It is important to understand who their contacts are going to be and how they plan to oversee their investment. Ideally, the family owners want someone who can pay attention to them at the senior level and provide continuity in dialogue with the family.

◆ **The fund's investors.** Not all private equity funds are the same. The types of investors in the fund will often dictate the degree of flexibility and the terms of the investment. For instance, private equity funds whose investors are multifamily offices or individuals will typically have the largest degree of flexibility regarding investment terms as well as timing and structure of their exit.

♦ **Other capabilities.** What sorts of strategic guidance, board representation, or industry networking contacts can the partners provide? For example, Parthenon Capital, based in Boston, was a strategic consulting firm that branched into private equity. It obviously brings a deep strategic angle to investments.

TERMS

♦ **Structure of the investment.** Do the investors expect their stake to be in the form of common or preferred stock? What length of exit do they want? What kind of approvals would they require? What percent of ownership will they expect in exchange for the funds they invest in the company? Remember: transitional capital can be majority or minority capital. Will the deal come with control clauses that will allow the private equity fund to take control of the company if it doesn't perform at a certain level?

♦ **Board seats.** How many board seats will the investors want, and how active will they be on the board? What outsiders might they bring to the board in addition to one or two of their own representatives? What resources and experience—such as in technology or overseas contacts—do these outsiders bring to the table?

Because many private equity funds are competing for a finite number of investment opportunities, family businesses can be very choosy, and they might look for someone who can bring

Table 16   Prerequisites for a Successful Private Equity Transaction

◆ **A well-defined growth story and a plan to implement it.** Before seeking a private equity partner, a company must have a well-thought-out business plan that describes how the capital will be used and how that will translate into growth. The management team must be on board with the business plan and understand the methods by which they will be rewarded.
◆ **Clearly defined liquidity needs of the owners.** In structuring a transaction with a private equity partner, family businesses would be well served to identify and provide for the immediate and ongoing liquidity needs of the family owners. After the private equity partners have entered a company, they will define the liquidity opportunities for the family. They will want to see all or most of their capital going to finance growth—not shareholder liquidity.
◆ **An effective family governance structure.** Before bringing in a private equity investor, it's important to ensure that a family governance structure is in place and functioning well. The board or shareholders' assembly can help crystallize the family's goals and provide a strong interface with the private equity partner during the investment period.

more than the money. With careful due diligence and planning, a properly structured and prepared family business should have no trouble finding a private equity partner who can help meet its business, family, and liquidity goals.

Chapter 9

Summary

Financial management of the family business has entered a new era. In the past, business owners facing a capital or liquidity squeeze often felt they had very restricted choices once they ran out of debt capacity: limiting growth, selling out, or going public. Today, business owners have many new, less-drastic financial techniques at hand to weather financial transitions. Careful planning to meet capital and liquidity needs, often coupled with these techniques, can help the family business survive the many transitions in ownership, management, and strategy that must be made if it is to endure through the generations.

Important principles and patterns lay the foundation for capital and liquidity planning. To sustain family control, the business owner must plan to manage some financial pressures innate to family businesses. The business's need for capital and shareholders' need for liquidity must be kept in equilibrium to avoid liquidity crises. This delicate balance is illustrated by the family business triangle, which shows how family control can be lost if either capital or liquidity needs go unmanaged. Neglecting shareholder liquidity needs can cause a downward liquidity spiral, which can weaken the business and ultimately leave shareholders little choice but to sell or liquidate it.

Another fundamental principle in managing capital and liquidity needs is to understand and manage your cost of capital. Cultivating shareholder unity and understanding of the business and its strategy is an important requirement for keeping capital costs low. Satisfied, confident shareholders tend not to demand high current returns on their equity because they believe in the business's long-term potential. This condition, which we have named "the Family Effect," can significantly reduce the business's cost of capital and greatly increase its competitive advantage. Also, meeting shareholders' liquidity needs on a planned, sustainable basis can help keep them under control. If no liquidity is provided to shareholders, they are more likely to demand high current returns.

The perceived riskiness of the investment, the level of liquidity, and the Family Effect are major components that help determine family business shareholders' expectations of the rate of return they must receive. This interplay is summarized in the Family Shareholder Return Formula. As the formula shows, cultivating the Family Effect and planning for shareholder liquidity are not peripheral activities. They are fundamental to sustaining the core competitive advantage of the family business: low-cost, patient capital.

Finally, this book describes 22 financial situations that can help meet liquidity or capital needs. Some require outside capital and others do not. Some entail shifting from complete family ownership of the business to family control of the business, and others do not. But all, under the right circumstances, can help the business owner's family maintain control over decision making in order to make wise, well-timed choices about the future of the business and the family.

Index

The Authors

Craig E. Aronoff is Co-founder, Principal Consultant, and Chairman of the Board of the Family Business Consulting Group, Inc.; Founder of the Cox Family Enterprise Center; and current Professor Emeritus at Kennesaw State University. He invented and implemented the membership-based, professional-service-provider-sponsored Family Business Forum, which has served as a model of family business education for universities world-wide.

John L. Ward is Co-founder of the Family Business Consulting Group, Inc. He is Clinical Professor at the Kellogg School of Management and teaches strategic management, business leadership, and family enterprise continuity.

François M. de Visscher is President of de Visscher & Co., Founder of Family Capital Growth Partners, Co-founder of the Business Growth Alliance, and a director and shareholder of his own family's global enterprise, N.V. Bekaert S.A.

ADDITIONAL BESTSELLING BOOKS FO
YOUR FAMILY BUSINESS LIBRARY

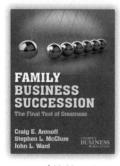

FAMILY BUSINESS SUCCESSION
The Final Test of Greatness

Craig E. Aronoff
Stephen L. McClure
John L. Ward

$23.00
978-0-230-11100-4

FAMILY BUSINESS GOVERNANCE
Maximizing Family and Business Potential

Craig E. Aronoff
John L. Ward

$23.00
978-0-230-11106-6

MAKING SIBLING TEAMS WORK
The Next Generation

Craig E. Aronoff
Joseph H. Astrachan
Drew S. Mendoza
John L. Ward

$23.00
978-0-230-11108-0

Keeping the Family Business Healthy
How to Plan for Continuing Growth, Profitability, and Family Leadership

JOHN L. WARD

$50.00
978-0-230-11121-9

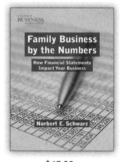

Family Business by the Numbers
How Financial Statements Impact Your Business

Norbert E. Schwarz

$45.00
978-0-230-11123-3

"Each Family Business Leadership publication is packed cover-to-cover with expert guidance, solid information and ideas that work."

—Alan Campbell, CFO, Campbell Motel Properties, Inc., Brea,

"While each volume contains helpful 'solutions' to the issues it covers, it is the guidance on how to tackle the process of addressing the different issues, and the emphasis on the benefits which can stem from the process itself, which make the Family Business publications of unique value to everyone involved in a family business—not just the owners."

—David Grant, Director (retired), William Grant & Sons L (distillers of Glenfiddich and other fine Scotch whiske